MAXnotes®

Mary Shelley's

Frankenstein

Text by
Kevin Kelly
(M.F.A., Columbia University)
Department of Communications
Andover College
Portland, Maine

Illustrations by
Karen Pica

Research & Education Association

What **MAXnotes**® *Will Do for You*

This book is intended to help you absorb the essential contents and features of Mary Shelley's *Frankenstein* and to help you gain a thorough understanding of the work. The book has been designed to do this more quickly and effectively than any other study guide.

For best results, this **MAXnotes** book should be used as a companion to the actual work, not instead of it. The interaction between the two will greatly benefit you.

To help you in your studies, this book presents the most up-to-date interpretations of every section of the actual work, followed by questions and fully explained answers that will enable you to analyze the material critically. The questions also will help you to test your understanding of the work and will prepare you for discussions and exams.

Meaningful illustrations are included to further enhance your understanding and enjoyment of the literary work. The illustrations are designed to place you into the mood and spirit of the work's settings.

The **MAXnotes** also include summaries, character lists, explanations of plot, and section-by-section analyses. A biography of the author and discussion of the work's historical context will help you put this literary piece into the proper perspective of what is taking place.

The use of this study guide will save you the hours of preparation time that would ordinarily be required to arrive at a complete grasp of this work of literature. You will be well prepared for classroom discussions, homework, and exams. The guidelines that are included for writing papers and reports on various topics will prepare you for any added work which may be assigned.

The **MAXnotes** will take your grades "to the max."

Dr. Max Fogiel
Program Director

Contents

> **Each Letter/Chapter includes List of Characters, Summary, Analysis, Study Questions and Answers, and Suggested Essay Topics.**

SECTION ONE

Introduction

The Life and Work of Mary Wollstonecraft Shelley

Mary Shelley dedicated her first novel, *Frankenstein or, The Modern Prometheus*, to her father, William Godwin. Godwin, a respected writer himself, was the author of two well-known books, *Political Justice* (1793) and *Caleb Williams* (1794). Godwin's work contained controversial philosophical ideas and critiques of society. His belief in the inherent decency of human beings influenced a number of the Romantic poets of the time. In 1797, he married Mary Wollstonecraft, a distinguished writer whose *A Vindication of the Rights of Women* was published in 1792. They had been married less than a year when Wollstonecraft died after giving birth to their daughter, Mary, who was born on August 30, 1797.

After Godwin remarried, Mary was raised by her stepmother, Mrs. Clairmont, a widow with two children of her own. Although Godwin had hoped to provide a stable family for his daughter, Mary had a difficult childhood, due in part to her contentious relationship with Clairmont. When Mary was 15, she moved into the home of the Baxters, who were friends of her father. It was at the Baxter's house, in May 1814, that she met Percy Bysshe Shelley, a notable young poet who was there visiting Godwin. Although Percy was already married, he and Mary fell in love. In June, they left England together to travel through Europe. On February 22, 1815, Mary gave birth to a premature child, who died three weeks later. Another child, William, was born in January 1816.

Five months later, Percy and Mary traveled to Switzerland where they rented a cottage for the summer. Their neighbors included their friend, Lord Byron, who had a home near Geneva. During a rainy spell, when the evenings were cold and damp, Mary, Percy, and Byron would gather in front of Byron's fireplace and entertain each other by reading German ghost stories. Inspired by the tales, the three friends agreed to each write a story similar to ones they had been reading. Although Percy and Byron never completed theirs, Mary went on to write a story that would eventually become the novel *Frankenstein*. The eventful year concluded in tragedy after Shelley's wife, Harriet, committed suicide, drowning herself on December 10, 1816. Percy and Mary were legally married three weeks later. Another son, Percy Florence, was born shortly after the wedding.

Mary's novel, *Frankenstein*, was published in 1818 and its success brought Mary considerable recognition. Five months after it was published, a friend wrote from England that the book was "universally known and read." But this success would soon be overshadowed by tragedies in the author's life. Two of her three children became ill and died—Clara on September 24, 1818, and William on June 7, 1819. Then, three years later on July 8, 1822, Percy Shelley drowned with two companions when his boat was caught in a heavy squall on the Bay of Spezia in Italy.

In spite of the unhappiness in her life, Mary Shelley continued to write. Her second novel, *Valperga*, was a success after it was published in 1823. Other works include *The Last Man* (1826), *The Fortunes of Perkin Warbeck, A Romance* (1830), *Lodore* (1835), and *Falkner* (1837). An account of her European travels in the 1840s was published in two volumes under the title *Rambles* in Germany (1844). She is also the author of two dramas, *Proserpine, A Mythological Drama in Two Acts*, and *Midas*, both written in the late 1820s, as well as a number of short stories and poems.

Shelley's only surviving child, Percy Florence, became Lord Shelley in 1844. He married a few years later and Mary lived comfortably with his family until her death, at the age of 54, on February 1, 1851.

Historical Background

Published in 1818, Mary Wollstonecraft Shelley's *Frankenstein or, The Modern Prometheus* added to the growing body of Romantic fiction published in the early 1800s. Shelley became one of the most influential writers of both Romantic and Gothic fiction, establishing, with *Frankenstein*, a new genre known today as science fiction.

Gothic romance often deals with mysterious and supernatural subjects. Gothic stories frequently take place in rugged, natural settings, near ancient castles or monasteries. The plots are suspenseful and usually deal with the forces of good and evil. One of the earliest works of Gothic fiction is Horace Walpole's *The Castle of Otranto* (1764).

In his novel, Walpole challenged the realistic style of the time by writing about the past and the subconscious. His Gothic romance is one of the earliest examples of the emerging romantic movement. Novels such as Ann Radcliffe's *Mysteries of Udolpho* (1794), Matthew Gregory Lewis's *The Monk* (1796), and William Godwin's *Caleb Williams* are other examples of the Gothic romance. American writers such as Nathaniel Hawthorne and Edgar Allan Poe also wrote in the Gothic style, which remained popular until the 1820s.

Romanticism was a separate intellectual and artistic movement that began in Europe in the middle of the eighteenth century. Romantics, who promoted the uniqueness of individual imagination and expression, believed in the interrelation of nature, spirituality, and humankind. The movement, which began in Germany, soon became popular in England as well. The lyrical ballads of William Wordsworth and Samuel Taylor Coleridge are generally considered to be the beginning of English romanticism. Many other writers, including Lord Byron, William Blake, John Keats, and Mary Shelley's husband, Percy Bysshe Shelley, wrote in the romantic style. Other notable fiction writers of the time include Jane Austen, whose *Pride and Prejudice* (1813) remains popular even today, and the poet Sir Walter Scott, who wrote his first novel, *Waverly*, in 1814.

In addition to their philosophical and spiritual concerns, the Romantic writers were also affected by the political events of the time. Beginning in 1789, the French Revolution had created an upheaval in Europe. Social reorganization lasted for the next 10 years as the rebellion continued to change the social structure and government of France. While many of the Romanticists favored the original principles of the revolution, which effectively abolished the French monarchy in favor of a more democratic system controlled by the middle classes, they were opposed to the extreme violence that helped bring about the changes. At the same time, England was also experiencing a profound transformation. The Industrial Revolution had made England a leading economic force in the world as mechanical power helped boost the country's production in every area of industry and manufacture.

After the French Revolution, France, which had aided the rebellious British colonies during the American Revolution, soon found itself engaged in a war with England. In 1804, Napoleon Bonaparte was crowned emperor of a revolutionary France still in flux. Within seven years, Napoleon had conquered all of Europe, from Spain to the Russian border with Prussia. The British, however, with the help of their powerful navy, remained unconquered. Then, in 1812, after Napoleon invaded Russia, a severe Russian winter cost France most of its army. A new European alliance, nurtured by British money and diplomacy, sprang up and France was defeated in Germany and Spain. Finally, in 1814, Napoleon surrendered and Britain, Russia, Austria, and Prussia drafted a peace treaty in Vienna. The following year, Napoleon returned from exile and raised a new army, but allied forces commanded by the British Duke of Wellington defeated Napoleon during a three-day battle at Waterloo in June 1815.

Mary Shelley, who was experiencing turmoil in her own family, was raised during this time of political unrest and violence. Her relationship with Percy Shelley was scandalous at the time, but she gained acceptance at an early age with the publication of *Frankenstein*. The book was as controversial as her affair with Shelley. Sir Walter Scott, writing in *Blackwood's* magazine, praised the novel as an "extraordinary tale" and Shelley as an author with "uncommon powers of poetic imagination." *Edinburgh* magazine said Shelley demonstrated a "mastery in harsh and savage delineations of passion," adding, however, that "it is one of those works...which we do not well see why it should have been written." The *Quarterly Review* praised the "highly terrific" language of the novel, but said "our taste and our judgment alike revolt at this kind of writing...it inculcates no lesson of conduct, manner, or morality;

it cannot mend, and will not even amuse its readers, unless their taste have been deplorably vitiated."

In spite of the mixed reviews it received, *Frankenstein* was a bestseller and would remain popular for generations. Mary Shelley became a respected author with numerous titles to her credit. It is the remarkable power of her first novel, though, that continues to inspire a host of horror stories and science fiction tales. Considering the book's lasting influence, it is hardly surprising that film adaptations of *Frankenstein* are still being made today.

Master List of Characters

Robert Walton—*An explorer who meets and cares for Victor Frankenstein while traveling in the Arctic; Walton writes to his sister, Margaret Saville, in England, relating Victor's horrible tale.*

The Creature—*Victor Frankenstein's "monster".*

Victor Frankenstein—*A young man, born in Switzerland, whose study of science and natural philosophy leads to his tragic creation of the monster.*

Alphonse Frankenstein—*Victor's father; a wealthy, influential man with humanitarian concerns.*

Beaufort—*Alphonse Frankenstein's friend and Caroline's father.*

Caroline Beaufort Frankenstein—*Victor's mother and Alphonse's wife; she dies shortly before Victor leaves for Ingolstadt.*

Elizabeth Lavenza—*A young woman who is adopted by the Frankenstein family; she marries Victor and is killed by the creature.*

Henry Clerval—*Victor's best friend and closest confidant; he is also killed by the creature.*

Ernest Frankenstein—*Victor's younger brother.*

William Frankenstein—*Victor's youngest brother; William is murdered by Victor's creature.*

Justine Moritz—*A young woman who lives with the Frankenstein family; Justine is falsely accused of killing William. She is tried and executed for the murder.*

M. Krempe—*Victor's philosophy professor at the University of Ingolstadt.*

M. Waldman—*Another professor who becomes Victor's mentor at Ingolstadt.*

Felix De Lacey—*A young peasant the creature observes living in a small cottage in the forest.*

Agatha De Lacey—*Felix's sister, who also lives in the cottage.*

M. De Lacey—*Felix's and Agatha's father; the creature tries to make friends with him.*

Safie—*A young Turkish woman who is Felix's fiancée.*

Safie's father—*A Turkish man Felix helps escape from prison.*

Mr. Kirwin—*A judicial magistrate who is in charge of Victor's case in Ireland.*

Daniel Nugent—*A witness in the murder case in Ireland.*

Nurse—*A woman who cares for Victor in prison.*

Magistrate—*A criminal judge in Geneva who listens to Victor's story about the creature.*

Summary of the Novel

Robert Walton, an explorer, describes his trip to the Arctic in letters to his sister, Margaret Saville, who lives in England. After discussing his preparations for the trip, one of Walton's letters informs Margaret that his ship is stuck and surrounded by ice. Walton then relates a strange event: As they looked out on the enormous ice field, Walton and his crew saw a gigantic man being pulled by a dogsled. The following day they discovered another, smaller man, desperately ill, adrift on a sheet of ice. Walton writes that he brought the man onto his ship, allowed him to rest, and attempted to nurse him back to health. After a week the man was able to talk and told Walton an incredible story.

The man's name is Victor Frankenstein, a young scientist born in Geneva, Switzerland. He is a member of a wealthy family concerned with humanitarian issues. Victor goes on to relate his story to Walton, who writes it down as Victor speaks, making a record of Victor's story, to be sent as a letter to Margaret Saville, Walton's sister.

Victor tells Walton that, as a boy, he was always fascinated by science and alchemy and he eventually attended the University of Ingolstadt to study natural science. At the university he focused all his attention on experiments designed to create life. After months of exhaustive study, Victor constructed a huge creature from parts of human cadavers. He then discovered a method of bringing it to life. However, when the creature opened its eyes, Victor was horrified by his monstrous-looking creation. He ran from his laboratory and became very ill and disoriented for almost two years. During this time, he believed that the creature must have perished.

After he recovered from his illness, as he prepared to return home to his family, Victor learned that William, his seven-year-old brother, had been murdered. Justine Moritz, a young woman the Frankenstein family had adopted, had been accused of the crime. But Victor refused to believe that Justine committed the murder. Instead, he suspected that his creature wasn't really dead, and was responsible for the horrible crime. However, after Victor returned to Geneva, Justine was tried, found guilty, and hanged.

Victor explains to Walton that he felt responsible for William's murder and Justine's execution. Guilt-ridden and desperate to be alone, he climbed into the mountains, where he encountered the creature. The creature told Victor that he had survived for the past two years, hiding out in the woods and eating nuts and berries. Lonely and miserable, he realized that he was repulsive to other human beings. In the forest, though, the creature discovered a gentle peasant family living in a cottage; by secretly observing them, the creature learned to read and write. Then, in his jacket pocket, the creature found Victor's journal and read of the experiments that led to his creation. Enraged, he concluded that it was Victor Frankenstein who was responsible for his misery.

After relating his story, the creature demanded that Victor recreate his experiment and construct another creature. The creature explained he was desperate for a companion who would not find him repulsive. If Victor does as he asks, he will go away with the new creature and never bother Victor again. Although wary of the proposal, Victor says he reluctantly agreed to the creature's request.

Victor tells Walton that he set up a new laboratory in Scotland and began the work of creating a companion for the creature. But he was haunted by the thought that this new monster might be more evil than the original, and he was terrified at the idea of the two creatures creating a new, horrible race of beings. So instead of completing his task, Victor destroyed his work before giving life to the new creation. But the original creature was watching Victor in his laboratory. Furious, he swore revenge, vowing to torment Victor for the rest of his life. Later that night the creature strangled Victor's best friend, Henry Clerval.

Several weeks later, Victor married Elizabeth Lavenza, a girl who was adopted by his family, and with whom Victor had always been in love. But after Victor and Elizabeth marry, the creature appeared on their wedding night and strangled Elizabeth to death. Grief-stricken over the death of Elizabeth, Alphonse Frankenstein, Victor's father, died a few months later. In utter despair, Victor vowed to pursue the creature and destroy it. He chased the monster for months, finally arriving in the Arctic where he met Walton and his expedition.

Having finished his story, Victor Frankenstein dies on Walton's ship. Walton ends the tale in additional letters to his sister, telling her that the night Victor died, the creature entered Victor's room and lamented his death. He then told Walton he planned to build a huge fire and burn himself to death. Before Walton could respond, the creature jumped from the ship and landed on a floating slab of ice. Walton concludes his final letter, telling Margaret that the creature was carried out to sea, where he disappeared into the darkness.

Estimated Reading Time

The Pennyroyal edition of *Frankenstein or, The Modern Prometheus* is 237 pages long with illustrations. While the novel is of average length, some of the language is dated and the sentences and paragraphs are rather long. The plot is complicated, and the narrative is unusual—related as a series of stories within stories and letters. It may be difficult for some readers to fully comprehend the entire text during a first reading. The average reader might want to divide his or her reading time into four or five sessions of two to three hours each, completing three to five chapters in each sitting.

Frankenstein or, The Modern Prometheus

Volume One: Letters One through Four

New Characters:

Robert Walton: *an explorer who writes to his sister Margaret in England; he encounters Victor Frankenstein on the Arctic ice and later records his horrible story*

The Creature: *a huge figure Walton sees traveling in a dogsled on the ice; later we learn that this is the "monster" created by Victor Frankenstein*

Victor Frankenstein: *a young scientist, unidentified by Walton in these letters, who is hunting for the monster he created*

Summary

Letter One

    The novel begins with a series of letters written by Robert Walton, a young English explorer, to his sister, Margaret Saville. Walton's first letter, written from St. Petersburg on "December 11, 17—" describes his plans for an Arctic expedition. He has been preparing for the voyage for six years, gathering information about the Arctic, and training himself physically so that he will be able to endure the harsh climate of the region. Walton also describes his youthful passion for literature. As a young man he had wanted to be a poet, but, after writing for a year, he considered himself a "failure" and he abandoned thoughts of a literary career. When he inherited a fortune from his cousin, he began to plan his Arctic expedition. Walton tells Margaret that he will begin his voyage in June.

Letter Two

On March 28, Walton informs his sister that he has found a crew for his expedition and they are ready to embark on their voyage. He is in a seaport called Archangel, excited at the prospect of his adventure, but he is lonely and longs to meet someone who shares his interests and intellectual curiosity. Walton hopes the man he hired to be the ship's master will turn out to be such a friend. Walton describes this man as being gentle and compassionate, and still recovering from a difficult romance with a young woman he was in love with but couldn't marry. The man had sacrificed himself, allowing the young woman to marry someone else; he also gave her lover land and money because the man was too poor to win the consent of the woman's father. Although it was an honorable deed, the ship's master continues to suffer for it.

In this letter, Walton also refers to Coleridge's "The Rime of the Ancient Mariner," a poem about a sailor who kills a friendly albatross. The mariner is tormented for this act until he repents and mystical forces finally bring his ship back home. Mary Shelley will mention this poem again later in the novel.

Letter Three

On July 7, Walton is at sea, heading for the Arctic region. His ship is encountering huge floating sheets of ice, but Walton is undeterred, excited by the adventure and determined to continue until he achieves his goal.

Letter Four

This last letter contains three separate entries, beginning on August 5. Walton's ship is stranded, surrounded by ice. As he and his crew survey the situation, they see a huge man in the distance,

being pulled on a dogsled. Later that day, the ice breaks and the ship is able to sail again. The following morning, the crew finds another man in a dogsled, trapped on a floating sheet of ice. The man is starving and nearly frozen to death, but he won't come aboard the ship until Walton tells him where the expedition is headed.

The man is half-delirious, but he begins to recover after a few days. Walton describes him as looking slightly mad. He says his guest is good-natured, although he appears to be very sad. The man has little to say until Walton tells him about the huge figure he saw traveling on the dogsled. The man is suddenly very alert, asking Walton many questions about the man and the direction he was headed. Walton is curious to know more about this giant figure, but he doesn't press the issue. Walton understands that the man he rescued is filled with grief and remorse. He tells Margaret that he has begun to love the man "like a brother," but, he says, the man's "constant and deep grief fills me with sympathy and compassion."

Walton writes the second part of the letter on August 13. Now Walton feels even greater affection for his new passenger, whose health continues to improve. The man begins to spend time on deck. He is still reluctant to explain the reasons he is looking for the other man. When Walton speaks to the man about his desire to find a good, understanding friend, the man says he understands. He tells Walton, sadly, he once had a friend like that himself, but now the friend is gone and he has nothing left.

Walton writes again on August 19. The man offers to tell Walton his story. Walton decides to make notes; he begins to record the man's experiences, writing them in the first person.

Analysis

Mary Shelley uses the device of Walton's letters to Margaret Saville at the outset of the novel to set a realistic tone for what is otherwise a completely fantastic story. Robert Walton is introduced as a pragmatic man, concerned with facts and the practical matters of his expedition. But he is also a Romantic adventurer, eager for the rewards of new experiences and sensitive to human emotions. Walton is established as a reliable reporter, so his description of his passenger as an honest, sincere man, makes his bizarre story more believable. Walton and his crew also serve as witnesses to the story when they catch a glimpse of the gigantic figure traveling on the ice.

Walton and his passenger share a common bond in their Romantic natures. Both men desire to explore the unknown and are inspired by grand ideas. There is also a strong emotional tie between the two, and they are both quite sensitive and sympathetic towards each other. For the Romantic writer, art and emotion are indelibly linked: art should not only express emotional concerns, but it should also have a strong influence on the emotions of those experiencing that art. Both Victor and Walton are typical Romantic characters. Victor immediately understands Walton's need for a close, spiritual friend. Walton is very aware of the terrible sadness that envelops his guest; he feels a kinship towards him, believing him to be a person of great intuition and judgment. Walton's description of the sad love affair of the ship's master is another example of his Romantic outlook. The ship master sacrifices himself for love, a pure ideal, and Walton is touched by this gesture.

Walton and his new passenger are alike in other ways. They are both sensitive, compassionate men who began their respective adventures with lofty visions, excited at the thought of the great discoveries they intend to make. They were both willing to endure great hardship in order to achieve their goals, and they were single-minded in the pursuit of their objectives. Walton, however, has yet to reach his destination; the other man is at the end of his journey. As Victor relates his story, Walton will hear how this man's quest brought him the most terrible misfortune.

Study Questions

1. What does Robert Walton hope to accomplish on his voyage?

2. How did Walton prepare himself for the expedition?

3. What did Walton read for the first 14 years of his life?

4. How old is Robert Walton?

5. Why did the ship's master decide not to get married?

6. How far is the ship from land when Walton sees the gigantic figure in the dogsled?

7. How does Walton describe his expedition when his new passenger asks about the ship's destination?

8. How does Walton feel about the man he rescues?

9. Why is the man Walton rescues traveling alone on the ice?

10. How does Walton feel about hearing his new friend's story?

Answers

1. Walton wants to visit, and walk upon, a part of the world that has never been seen before.

2. Walton prepared by going without food and sleep. He also endured cold temperatures. He worked on whaling ships during the day, and then studied all night.

3. As a child and as a young man, Walton read his uncle Thomas's books of voyages.

4. Walton is 28 years old.

5. The fiancée of the ship's master loved another man. He let her go because he wanted her to be happy.

6. Walton believes he is hundreds of miles from land when he sees the dogsled.

7. Walton tells the man he is on a "voyage of discovery towards the northern pole."

8. Walton says he loves him like a brother, and feels sympathy and compassion for him.

9. The man says, "To seek one who fled from me."

10. Walton is grateful that the man will tell his story, but he worries that telling it will cause the man renewed grief.

Suggested Essay Topics

1. Why do you think Robert Walton is so eager to visit such a hostile environment?

2. Discuss the similarities between Robert Walton and Victor Frankenstein, the man he rescues. Why does Walton feel such compassion for Victor, a total stranger?

3. Why is Walton so impressed with the shipmaster's actions regarding his fiancée?

4. What Romantic concepts do the characters of Victor and Walton illustrate?

Volume One: Chapters One and Two

New Characters:

Alphonse Frankenstein: *Victor's father*

Beaufort: *Alphonse's close friend and Caroline's father*

Caroline Beaufort Frankenstein: *Alphonse's wife and Victor's mother*

Elizabeth Lavenza: *Victor's adopted sister*

Henry Clerval: *Victor's closest friend*

Ernest Frankenstein: *Victor's brother*

William Frankenstein: *Victor's youngest brother*

M. Krempe: *an arrogant professor at the University of Ingolstadt who ridicules Victor*

M. Waldman: *a friendly professor who advises Victor to study modern science*

Summary

Robert Walton records Victor's story, writing his words in the first person: Victor Frankenstein (who has yet to reveal his name) was born in Geneva, Switzerland. He grew up a member of a wealthy, influential family; his father, Alphonse Frankenstein, was involved in politics. One of Alphonse's closest friends was a man named Beaufort, who had been a successful merchant for years until he lost his business, became sick and impoverished, and eventually died.

Beaufort's daughter, Caroline, had taken care of her father until his death. She worked at a simple job, plaiting straw, in order to support her father and herself. Before Beaufort died, Alphonse found him living with Caroline in a miserable hut. Although Beaufort was ashamed of his situation, Alphonse did what he could to care for him until he died. After her father's death, Alphonse took care of Caroline and eventually married her. Alphonse had long admired Caroline's virtues; he wanted to provide a comfortable home for her, and give her the happy life he felt she deserved but had long been denied.

After they were married, Alphonse and Caroline traveled extensively. Their son was born in Geneva, and the narrator was for several years their only child. The Frankensteins were very concerned with the plight of poor people they encountered around the world. In Italy, during a visit to Milan, Alphonse and Caroline adopted Elizabeth Lavenza, a beautiful peasant baby with striking golden hair. Elizabeth was loved by everyone who knew her, and Victor, who had been an only child, grew up feeling a special affection for her. Several years later, Alphonse and Caroline had another child.

Victor describes his childhood and his insatiable curiosity about the natural world around him: Attending school in Geneva, Victor, who is something of a loner, becomes best friends with another boy, Henry Clerval. Victor and Henry share the same scientific and philosophical interests. Victor is intrigued by natural philosophy after reading the works of Cornelius Agrippa. His father, however, does not approve of Agrippa and he tells Victor that Agrippa's writings are nothing but "trash." Victor is confused by his father's reaction, since Alphonse doesn't bother to say why he is dismissing this scientist. Later on, Victor tells us, he realized that the ancient principles of Agrippa had been "entirely exploded" by the modern system of science, and he wishes his father had taken the time to explain this to him. But for the present, Victor continues to pursue his study of Agrippa, along with the works of Magnus and Paracelsus.

When Victor is 15 he witnesses a violent thunderstorm and watches a bolt of lightning destroy a great old oak tree. This incident excites his curiosity, and he begins to study electricity, galvanism, and other natural phenomena while helping his father instruct his younger brothers, Ernest and William. He describes William, the youngest, as "the most beautiful little fellow." Victor says

this was a happy time in his life; he was enjoying his studies and everyone in his family loved each other and got along well. When he is 17, Victor enrolls in the University of Ingolstadt. He is excited at the idea of going away to study, but he becomes upset when he learns that his friend, Henry Clerval, won't be joining him. Then, before he leaves for the university, Elizabeth comes down with scarlet fever. Caroline nurses her back to health, but in the process becomes deathly ill with the disease herself. Her last wish is for Victor and Elizabeth to marry. Caroline's death deeply affects Victor and he has difficulty accepting that she is really gone. Victor departs for Ingolstadt with mixed emotions. He is very sad to be leaving his friends and family, and uncertain about being on his own.

At the university, Victor meets Professor M. Krempe, a distinguished instructor who teaches natural philosophy. Krempe does not approve of Victor's course of study and ridicules his favorite authors. Victor is disturbed by his encounter with Krempe, but is determined to continue with his studies. He seeks out another professor, M. Waldman, who is an understanding and helpful man. He encourages Victor to study modern science and to learn from science's most recent, exciting discoveries if he wants to penetrate the vast mysteries of nature. Victor tells us his meeting with M. Waldman was a memorable one, and it was a day that "decided my future destiny."

Analysis

Victor's happy childhood and ideal family life provides a stark contrast to the previous scenes aboard Walton's ship. Although we do not yet know why Victor is in the Arctic, it becomes apparent that a terrible tragedy has befallen him. From the warmth and comfort of his father's house, surrounded by friends and family, Victor has somehow ended up alone, half-frozen and emaciated, drifting on a sheet of ice in pursuit of a huge and still, to us, mysterious individual.

Victor's family is described in ideal terms, with loving parents and siblings who care for and enjoy each other. Victor's parents are also humanitarians, using their wealth and status to help those who are less fortunate than themselves. When Caroline dies, Victor is confronted with death for the first time, and it is an experience that will help propel him towards his bold experiments. His great love for his mother, and his inability to accept her death, provide a strong motivation for him to begin his exploration of the great questions of life and death.

Victor's friendship with Walton also takes on an added significance, echoing his feelings for Henry Clerval and Elizabeth, as well as his father's close relationship with Beaufort. Victor has already told Walton about the close friend he had and lost. Deep friendships, a classic Romantic concept (along with concern for the poor and less fortunate), occur throughout the novel and are constantly threatened by either natural phenomena or by Victor's creation, a being who comes to understand how important close relationships are to humans. The creature also will learn how to use those relationships to exact the most effective method of revenge. When the Frankensteins are hurt because of Victor's experiment, the tragedy, and Victor's suffering, is even greater because of the damage to his benevolent family.

Victor's intensive study of the scientists Agrippa, Magnus, and Paracelsus reveals his strong interest in alchemy and the natural sciences. Alchemy is an ancient science concerned with the transformation of base metals, such as lead, into gold. Alchemists also sought cures for diseases as a way to indefinitely prolong life. They were often associated with magicians and necromancers, but their practices remained very different. While necromancers might call on a demon or evil spirit in their work, alchemists believed that the key to understanding was within the mind of the practitioners themselves. Instead of chants and ceremonies, alchemists used substances from nature, mixing and heating them in various combinations, all in an effort to achieve a profound scientific knowledge. Like the necromancers, however, alchemists did believe that individual practitioners should be pure in spirit, devoted to a worthy cause. Both were seeking revelations about nature and existence. These pure ideals were also a part of the Romantic tradition.

Victor's early research into the work of the alchemists is an indication of his interest in discovering the principles of life and death. He is beginning his search for a God-like knowledge, a panacea to cure the ills of humankind. This type of fundamental

knowledge, and the possible disastrous consequences of acquiring such knowledge, were also of great interest to the Romanticists.

Study Questions

1. How did Victor's father spend his "younger days"?
2. While Victor was intrigued by science as a child, what were Elizabeth's chief interests?
3. What did Henry Clerval write when he was nine years old?
4. Where does Victor first come across the works of Agrippa?
5. What does Victor witness during the thunderstorm?
6. Why doesn't Henry Clerval attend the university with Victor?
7. What subject does Professor M. Krempe teach?
8. How does M. Waldman react when he hears the names of Agrippa and Paracelsus?
9. Before he leaves for the university, what does Victor hope to accomplish with his scientific studies?
10. According to Professor Waldman, what have the "modern masters" learned about blood and air?

Answers

1. He was "perpetually occupied by the affairs of his country."
2. Elizabeth was concerned with the "aerial creations of the poets." Victor explains that while he sought to discover the secrets of the world, Elizabeth thought of the world as a "vacancy, which she sought to people with imaginations of her own."
3. Henry wrote a fairy tale that delighted all his friends.
4. Victor comes across the works of Agrtippa at an inn near the baths of Thonon.
5. Victor witnesses a bolt of lightning that strikes and destroys a tree.

6. Henry's father wants him to join the family business.

7. Krempe teaches natural philosophy.

8. He smiles in a friendly way, without showing any contempt.

9. Victor wants to learn how to "banish disease from the human frame, and render man invulnerable to any but a violent death."

10. Waldman says they have "discovered how the blood circulates, and the nature of the air we breathe."

Suggested Essay Topics

1. Victor is deeply affected by Caroline's death. Discuss Victor's reaction to his mother's death and the influence it has on his scientific studies.

2. Discuss Victor's friendship with Henry Clerval and compare it to his father's relationship with Beaufort.

3. What is "modern science" as explained by M. Waldman, and how does it differ from the theories of Agrippa and the other scientists Victor studies?

Volume One: Chapters Three, Four, and Five

New Character:

Justine Moritz: *a young woman living with the Frankenstein family*

Summary

Under the guidance of M. Waldman, Victor dedicates himself to the study of natural science. He remains at the university for two years, completely absorbed in his studies, and becomes fascinated with the "structure of the human frame, and, indeed, any animal endued with life. Whence, I often asked myself, did the principle of life proceed?" Victor realizes that this is a "bold question" but he is determined to find the answer. He wonders "how many things are we upon the brink of becoming acquainted, if cowardice or carelessness did not restrain our inquiries." Victor understands that such an inquiry into the cause and nature of life will be extremely difficult, but he applies himself to his studies with an "almost supernatural enthusiasm." However, during this time, he neglects his family and friends and doesn't contact anyone in Geneva.

Working on his own, Victor makes an exhaustive study of the process of death and decay in the human body. Eventually he discovers a method of generating life in nonliving matter. Although excited by his discovery—"a light so brilliant and wondrous, yet so simple"—Victor is nevertheless wary of the knowledge he now possesses. He feels that it could be dangerous, but he continues to work, convinced that he will be able to create life and ultimately help humankind. He hopes that one day he will be able to restore life to human beings who have died. To prove his theories, Victor decides to assemble a huge human figure, eight feet tall, that he will eventually bring to life. He believes that working on a larger scale will better allow him to experiment more effectively on normally minuscule parts of the human body.

Victor begins his work by collecting body parts from graveyards and charnel houses. Working alone, he becomes obsessed with his experiment and completely cuts himself off from everyone he knows. Finally, after months of hard work, Victor finishes his work and he infuses life into his creation. However, when the gigantic creature opens its eyes, Victor is immediately horrified by the result. He finds the creature repulsive, with "yellow skin" stretched tightly over its muscles and arteries, a horrible grin, and watery eyes. After working for nearly two years, on what he thought would be a beautiful creation, Victor realizes "the beauty of the dream vanished, and breathless horror and disgust filled my heart." Unable to bear the sight of his creature, Victor rushes from the room and collapses, exhausted from the shock. The creature comes to his room and tries to speak to him, but Victor runs out of his house, desperate to get away from the "thing" he has created.

As the distraught Victor roams through the city, terrified of running into the creature, he meets his good friend Henry Clerval, who has traveled from Geneva to see him. Henry and the Frankenstein family haven't heard from Victor in months and they are

very concerned about him. Victor is overjoyed to see his friend; for a moment he is able to forget his troubles. But when they return to Victor's house, Victor begins ranting about his creation and Henry thinks his friend is ill with a fever. Victor becomes delirious and Henry takes care of him for several months. The creature has disappeared and Henry is unaware of Victor's experiments.

When Victor recovers, he receives a letter from Elizabeth. She describes her activities at home and other family news, including information about Justine Moritz, a young woman who has recently become part of the Frankenstein family after her own family died. Victor greatly enjoys the letter and longs to see his home and family again.

Over the summer, as Victor makes plans to return to Geneva, Clerval becomes acquainted with Victor's friends and teachers at the university. Victor's professors all praise his remarkable academic achievements. In the fall, an unexpected period of harsh winter weather forces a change in plans, and Victor and Henry have to postpone their departure. They remain in Ingolstadt for the winter where Victor fully recovers from his exhaustion and the shock of his horrible experiment. He enjoys Henry's company enormously and when spring arrives, Victor is feeling happy and content.

Analysis

Victor never actually explains how the creature is brought to life, although he hints at the use of various chemical methods combined with the power of electricity. During the eighteenth and nineteenth centuries, much of the scientific information we understand today was as yet unknown. Early scientists, however, were making startling discoveries about the natural world and were studying phenomena such as lightning and electricity. There were also great advances in the understanding of human anatomy and physiology. Many of the scientists of the time were fascinated with the power of electricity and its effect on animals. Experiments were also being conducted on human corpses, specifically the bodies of executed murderers. In 1803, Dr. J. C. S. Carpue attempted, unsuccessfully, to revive a hanged man using a powerful electric current, one of several such experiments during that time. Although

Victor's creation may sound fantastic today, we should remember that Mary Shelley's novel was imagined during an era of great scientific discovery and curiosity. The Gothic style in which the novel is written also makes the use of gruesome, supernatural elements acceptable. The full title of Mary Shelley's novel is *Frankenstein or, The Modern Prometheus*. It is important to note that Frankenstein is not the creature itself, but Victor, the scientist who created the creature out of a desire to help humankind. In Greek mythology, Prometheus stole fire from the gods and created man from clay. His actions greatly offended Zeus, who then created Pandora, a woman who became the guardian of all the world's woes. In *Prometheus Bound*, a play by Aeschylus, Zeus chains Prometheus to a rock on Mount Caucasus. Each day an eagle eats Prometheus's liver, which grows back at night; when the eagle returns the next day, the torture begins again. Prometheus is punished by Zeus for giving the gifts of intellect, love, and compassion to humankind. Mary Shelley's husband, Percy, also dealt with the Prometheus myth when he wrote *Prometheus Unbound*, a four-act drama. Shelley's play uses the classical myth to explore the idea that love and goodness will ultimately triumph over human selfishness and evil. In these chapters, we see that Victor is not only creating life, but he is, at the same time, trying to discover a way to overcome life's inevitable consequence, death. We will see, however, that in Mary Shelley's work, Victor is not punished for trying to help human beings. Instead, his endless misery stems from his rejecting and abandoning his own creation.

After he brings the creature to life, Victor is horrified by the creature. The creature only wants to be accepted by Victor; after Frankenstein faints and collapses on his bed, the creature tries to communicate with him, but Victor runs away, leaving the creature hopelessly alone, stranded in a confusing, hostile environment. Victor's action stands in sharp contrast to the love and support his close friend, Clerval, offers him. Harold Bloom notes that "Frankenstein's tragedy stems not from his Promethean excess but from his own moral error, his failure to love; he abhorred his creature, became terrified, and fled his responsibilities." (Bloom, 6)

Study Questions

1. After he begins his study of natural philosophy, how does Victor feel about M. Waldman?

2. How tall does Victor plan to make his creature?

3. How does Victor describe himself after his months of study?

4. In what month does Victor finally complete his experiment?

5. What color is the creature's hair and lips?

6. After he brings the creature to life, who does Victor dream about meeting in Ingolstadt?

7. What does the creature do when he visits Victor in his bedroom?

8. As he wanders the streets of Ingolstadt, what poem does Victor quote?

9. After he recovers from his illness, how does Victor react when he finally sees his laboratory instruments again?

10. When Henry invents tales to amuse Victor, what kind of writers does he imitate?

Answers

1. Victor says he regards Waldman as "a true friend."

2. He plans to construct a figure that is eight feet tall.

3. Victor says he is pale and emaciated after months of study.

4. He brings the creature to life "on a dreary night of November."

5. Black. Victor describes the creature as having flowing hair of "lustrous black" and "straight black lips."

6. Victor dreams about meeting Elizabeth in Ingolstadt.

7. The creature grins and holds out his hand to Victor.

8. He quotes lines from Coleridge's "Rime of the Ancient Mariner," the same poem that was referred to earlier in Robert Walton's second letter to his sister.

9. He becomes nervous and suffers from renewed anxiety at the thought of his experiment.

10. Henry imitates the style of Persian and Arabic writers.

Suggested Essay Topics

1. Why do you think Victor created such a horrible-looking creature? Did he realize what he was doing? Explain your answer.

2. What are some of the characteristics of the Gothic novel, and how does Mary Shelley use them in these chapters?

3. Victor tells us that his friend Clerval's imagination was "too vivid for the minutiae of science." What does he mean by this?

Volume One: Chapters Six and Seven

Summary

Before he leaves Ingolstadt, Victor receives a letter from his father, Alphonse, relating the dreadful news that his youngest brother, William, was murdered while the family was on an outing in Plainpalais. During a hike, William wandered off and was discovered hours later, strangled, the killer's handprints imbedded in his neck. Alphonse is terribly upset and he asks Victor to come home to the "house of mourning." Victor is horrified by the news and returns to Geneva immediately.

On his journey home, Victor is sad and fearful. As he is crossing the Alps near Mont Blanc, a vicious storm suddenly appears "at once in various parts of the heavens." Victor looks at the sky and cries out, "William, dear angel! This is thy funeral, this thy dirge!" At that moment he sees a gigantic figure illuminated by a bolt of lightning. Victor instantly recognizes the figure as the creature he brought to life, and he instinctively realizes that it was the creature who killed his brother William. Victor feels an enormous weight of responsibility for having created this "depraved wretch" who delights in death and misery.

When Victor arrives home, he learns that Justine Moritz has been arrested for William's murder. Victor and Elizabeth, however, refuse to believe that Justine is the killer and the family is convinced that she will be found not guilty. During the trial, however, incriminating evidence is introduced, facts that cast doubt on Justine's claim of innocence. In addition to being seen near the scene of the crime, authorities found a locket belonging to William in Justine's pocket. Justine claims she was searching for William herself that night and ended up sleeping in a barn outside the city. She doesn't remember ever taking William's locket, and she doesn't know how it ended up in her pocket. Several character witnesses, including Elizabeth, testify in Justine's behalf, but at the end of the trial, Justine is convicted of the murder and sentenced to death.

Both Victor and Elizabeth are terribly distraught. When they visit Justine in jail, she reveals that, after her conviction, she finally confessed to the murder so that her priest would grant her absolution. She says the priest had "besieged" her since the trial, threatening her with "excommunication and hell fire" unless she confessed. However, she tells Victor and Elizabeth that she is completely innocent. But the sentence is carried out and Justine is hanged the following morning; the Frankenstein family is unable to save her. Although he won't tell anyone about his horrible experiment, Victor is certain the creature committed the crime. He blames himself for the deaths of William and Justine.

Analysis

Although, at this point, the true identity of William's murderer remains a mystery, Victor's intuitive suspicion that the creature committed the murder compounds the tragedy of the deaths of his brother and Justine. Victor had hoped to put his experiment at Ingolstadt behind him, but his irresponsible behavior following the creation of his "demon" continues to haunt him. As sure as he is of Justine's innocence, however, Victor refuses to step forward to save her. He never discusses his creation with anyone, nor does he voice his suspicions about the murder to the court. Although he is unwilling to implicate himself in the death of his brother, Frankenstein is convinced that his creature is responsible for the deaths.

Victor also believes that the creature is inherently evil and malicious. His one brief encounter with the creature, two years earlier when he brought it to life, has somehow led him to this conclusion. Later, Frankenstein will learn more about this "monster" that he is responsible for, but he will remain steadfast in his opinion of the dark nature of his creation. Victor is willing to accept responsibility for the creature's existence, but he fails to understand that his own actions after the creature's "birth," as well as the treatment of the creature by other human beings, are responsible for the creature's malevolent behavior.

In Volume One, the story was mainly concerned with Victor's development as a scientist and his obsessive quest to create a living being. Shelley's use of Walton's letters as a framing device for the novel allow us to glimpse the ending of the story at the very beginning; we have a hint of what is to come, and while Victor's life begins full of hope and promise, we have already seen evidence, on Walton's ship, that Victor's actions may lead to a dreadful conclusion. Victor's own innate sense of foreboding failed to prevent him from completing his experiment. Now we begin to see the consequences of his actions.

Study Questions

1. Who is Ernest Frankenstein?

2. Why did William hide from Ernest in Plainpalais?

3. Why did Elizabeth feel responsible for William's murder?

4. How long has Victor been away from home, studying at Ingolstadt?

5. When Victor sees the creature in the Alps, why doesn't he pursue it?

6. How has Elizabeth changed in the six years since Victor has seen her?

7. How does Justine look and behave during her trial?

8. How did Justine react when she was shown William's body?

9. Whom does Victor consider to be the "true murderer" of William?

10. How does Elizabeth feel after she visits Justine in prison?

Answers

1. Ernest is Victor's and William's brother. He returned alone after he and William went off to play.

2. William and Ernest were playing hide-and-go-seek.

3. Elizabeth had given William the locket. She assumed the murderer killed William to get the locket, however, she believes Justine is innocent.

4. Victor has been away for six years.

5. The creature would be impossible to catch. Victor has seen it bound up Mount Saleve with tremendous speed and agility.

6. Elizabeth has grown up and become an "uncommonly lovely" woman.

7. Victor describes Justine as being calm and tranquil during the trial, and "confident in innocence."

8. She became hysterical and was ill for several days.

9. Victor thinks of himself as the "true murderer."

10. Although Justine has been condemned to death, Elizabeth is relieved to learn that Justine is really innocent. If Justine had been guilty, Elizabeth would have felt terrible anguish at being deceived by someone she loved and trusted.

Suggested Essay Topics

1. After Justine is accused of William's murder, why do you think Victor never tells anyone about the creature?

2. Explain why Justine confesses to the crime, even though she is innocent.

3. Discuss Victor's experience with lightning and Shelley's use of it when Victor sees the creature.

Volume Two: Chapters One and Two

Summary

Following the deaths of William and Justine, Victor experiences a feeling of profound despair. He created the monster and now he blames himself for the deaths of two innocent people. Alphonse tries to console his son to no avail. Victor's grief is compounded by remorse and his father doesn't understand all of the awful reasons for his son's depression.

The family moves to their house in Belrive, a country estate outside Geneva. At night, Victor often sails alone in the nearby lake, reflecting on his misery. He is so unhappy that he contemplates suicide and "often" considers drowning himself in the lake, but he realizes that this act would only cause his family, and especially Elizabeth, more suffering. Victor continues to live in fear that his creature will strike again, causing more pain and horror. He tells us: "My abhorrence of this fiend cannot be conceived." Elizabeth is also having a difficult time accepting the deaths of William and Justine. She is no longer the innocent, happy person she was before the tragedy. She knows that somewhere William's murderer is walking around freely because Justine was punished for his crime.

Victor is in such torment that he believes his only consolation would be to find the monster and take revenge. But he accompanies his family on a trip to the mountains, hoping the magnificent natural surroundings will help him forget the terrible incident. The Frankensteins travel to Chamonix, a small town in the French Alps at the foot of Mont Blanc. There Victor finds a small measure of peace, taking solace in the beautiful scenery that helps distract him from his painful memories. One day, as he hikes into the mountains, climbing over loose rocks and scrambling up dangerous ledges, Victor thinks he would be better off if he were an animal, incapable of human thought and concerns.

Victor continues his climb and after several hours makes it to a summit where he rests, looking out over the mountains and a huge glacier that reminds him of the sea. As Victor enjoys the view, allowing himself a small moment of pleasure, suddenly, in the distance, the monster appears. He leaps towards Victor with incredible speed, then stops and addresses his horrified creator. The

creature tells Victor that he understands how much Victor hates him, and he knows that Victor would like to destroy him. The monster describes himself as being "miserable beyond all living things." He will never be able to experience the happiness he has seen humans enjoy. "Misery," he says, "made me a fiend." He asks Victor to listen to his story, reminding him that Victor is responsible for his existence. "I am thy creature," he says. If Victor does as the creature asks, the creature promises to go away and leave Victor and his family in peace. Otherwise, the creature says, he will "glut the maw of death, until it be satiated with the blood of your remaining friends."

Victor finally agrees to listen to the creature. With a "heavy heart" he follows the creature across a field of ice to a small hut. Together they sit by a fire and Victor listens to his creature's story.

Analysis

Victor is now fully aware that he can no longer ignore his creation. After Justine is executed, Victor is divided between two emotional responses: the grief and depression that continue to plague him, and the desire for revenge. Tormented by the deaths of his loved ones, Victor considers the possibility that revenge against the creature may be the only cure for his despair. He chooses, for the moment, however, to visit the Alps with his family, hoping, along with his father, that the trip will restore his "serenity." It is interesting to note that Frankenstein's driving ambition resulted in a creation that is destroying his life. When he began his project, he hoped to gain an understanding of the life process, an ultimate knowledge that would benefit humankind. Instead, he created a monster that is a threat to himself, his family, and, in his opinion, the human race. We will come to learn, however, that the creature is a far different being than the vicious monster Victor imagines him to be.

When Victor agrees to go to the Alps, he is once again shirking his responsibility, denying what he did in his laboratory and refusing to admit it to others. He believes the creature is evil and the murderer of his brother; yet, although his other family members may be in imminent danger, he warns no one, hoping instead that the creature will disappear and choose not to strike again. But as

Victor seeks a peaceful refuge in the magnificent scenery of the Alps, the creature seeks him out, refusing to go on being ignored and rejected by Victor. Once again, Shelley uses the Romantic device of placing Victor in a rugged, natural setting, seeking comfort from the beautiful landscapes, as he continues to brood about his life and misfortunes. When he is in the mountains, or alone, sailing on the lake, Victor often considers suicide as he contemplates his dilemma. Here, Shelley follows another Romantic tradition, allowing this highly emotional character, in deep despair, to consider ending his own life. Ironically, Victor's thoughts of suicide contradict his youthful quest at Ingolstadt, when he was obsessed with finding a way to subvert death and create life.

Contrary to Victor's descriptions of him, the creature reveals himself to be an intelligent, emotional being. He is capable of discussing religious and philosophical issues as well as his own feelings and experiences. The creature knows that humans despise him because of his horrid appearance. When Frankenstein calls him a "Devil," the creature is not surprised. "I expected this reception," he says. "All men hate the wretched...." The creature fully understands his role in society and how he is viewed by others. His perception and understanding of human reaction is particularly keen, and he is appalled by Victor's rejection of him. "How dare you sport thus with life?" he asks Frankenstein, who can only respond with rage. Here, the creature is the reasonable one who only wants his creator to listen to him and try to understand him. Victor finally accepts the creature's proposal, telling us that he understood, at last, what the "duties of a creator towards his creature were," although he follows the creature with a "heavy heart."

Study Questions

1. Where does the Frankenstein family move to after Justine is executed?

2. How does Victor spend his time at Belrive?

3. When does Victor like to sail his boat?

4. Besides sailing, what else does Victor consider doing at the lake?

5. How do Victor and his family travel to Chamonix?

6. What is Victor looking at when the creature appears?

7. What does Victor call the creature when he first sees him?

8. What happens when Victor tries to attack the creature?

9. Why does Victor agree to listen to the creature's story?

10. What is the creature's mood when he enters the hut with Victor?

Answers

1. The family moves into their house in Belrive.

2. Victor sails his sailboat aimlessly, letting the wind blow him in any direction.

3. He usually sails at night, after his family has gone to sleep.

4. Victor thinks about committing suicide by drowning himself in the lake.

5. They travel first by carriage and later, as they enter the mountains, by mule.

6. Victor is looking at Mont Blanc and Montanvert, two mountains in the Alps.

7. Victor calls him "Devil!" and a "vile insect."

8. When Victor springs at the creature, the creature easily eludes him.

9. Victor is not only curious, but he is also moved by a strange compassion for the creature, and he feels a sense of duty because he is the monster's creator.

10. Victor says the creature is exultant.

Suggested Essay Topics

1. The creature tells Frankenstein: "misery made me a fiend." Do you think the creature's unhappiness justifies his murderous behavior? Explain your answer using examples from the text.

2. Victor contemplates suicide while sailing on the lake, and again when climbing the mountain. Discuss the change in Victor's personality from his university days.

Volume Two: Chapters Three, Four, and Five

New Characters:

Felix De Lacey: *a young peasant the creature observes living in a small cottage in the forest*

Agatha De Lacey: *Felix's sister who also lives in the cottage*

M. De Lacey: *Felix's and Agatha's father; the creature tries to make friends with him*

Safie: *a young Turkish woman who is Felix's fiancée*

Summary

Sitting in the hut by the fire, the creature relates his experiences during the two years since Victor created him. The creature tells Victor about the difficulties he had trying to cope with the strange feelings of his senses. Having never had the opportunity to mature in a normal way, the creature was overwhelmed by the many sensations he experienced when he was first brought to life. He also felt confused by Victor's rejection of him, by the bright daylight, and by the feelings of thirst and hunger that constantly plagued him. To escape the intense light, the creature ran and hid in a nearby forest, covering himself with Victor's clothes and, later, a cloak that he finds. He passed his first night in the forest, where he discovered the remains of a campfire. Drawn to the warmth, he plunged his hands into the fire and burned himself. The creature says the experience taught him about the enormous power of fire, along with the benefits of heat and light.

In the forest, surrounded by nature, the creature tells Victor that when he first heard the songs of birds, he found the sound "sweet and enticing." The creature continued to roam through the forest searching for food. When he came upon a small hut, he entered it and found a man preparing a meal. Although the creature meant no harm, the man fled in terror when he entered the hut, and the creature realized that his appearance must be horrible to human beings. The creature enjoyed the man's meal, then found more huts in a nearby village, which he thought was "miraculous" with its neat cottages, huts, and "stately houses." But the villagers were horrified when they saw the creature and they chased and beat him. He escaped into the forest, understanding that he would never be accepted by human beings.

The creature wandered through the forest and eventually came upon a small cottage with a crude shack attached to it. He moved into the shack, glad to find refuge from the cold, wet weather, and relieved to be hidden from the humans who abused him. The creature settled into his new home and soon discovered that he could observe the humans in the cottage by spying on them through a crack in the wall. Inside, he saw an old man living with a young couple. The creature noticed how kind these humans seemed, and how they enjoyed each other's company. He watched them play music, sing songs, and read books and poems together. The creature tells Victor he was amazed by this tranquil scene, although he perceived that the family was unhappy about something. Later, he discovered that they were very poor, although generous and willing to share their meager resources. The creature was moved by their kindness and performed services for them in secret, such as shoveling their snow at night when they slept

As the creature continued to observe the family, he learned that the couple were a brother and sister named Felix and Agatha. They called the old man "father." By watching the family, the creature also learned how to perform a variety of useful tasks, and he discovered the value of speech and the written word. The creature explains that he longed to talk to the family and wanted to learn from them, but he was sure they would be frightened of him. The creature was aware of how awful he looked because he had seen his reflection in a pool of water and was horrified by his own appearance. As he stared at his reflection, he compared himself to the "perfect forms" of the cottagers, and their "grace, beauty, and delicate complexions." Looking at himself in the pool, he became fully convinced that he was a "monster." This knowledge filled him with the "bitterest sensations of despondence and mortification."

In the spring, Felix's fiancée, a young woman named Safie, moved into the cottage. The creature observed them, learning more as Felix taught Safie about a variety of subjects. The creature came to admire knowledge, virtue, and "gentle manners"; however, the more he learned, the more he understood how hideous he was to others. He suffered from the acute pain of his isolation.

Analysis

Here again, Shelley uses the device of a story within a story to continue the series of first-person narratives. Remember that Victor is actually relating the creature's story to Walton who, in turn, is writing it down as a letter to his sister. Walton, who at the outset of the novel is introduced as an intelligent, rational man, serves as an objective reporter of a story that, as it develops, becomes increasingly fantastic.

The creature's first response to human beings is a benevolent one. His natural reaction is to feel sorry for them when they are suffering and cheerful when they are glad. He is even eager to help the peasant family because it makes him feel good. The creature also has a strong emotional reaction to nature. He is impressed by the beauty of the moon and enjoys hearing the "sweet" sounds of the birds in the forest. From reading and observation, he has learned important lessons about history, literature, and spirituality; and he has gained an understanding of human beings and their behavior. As the creature speaks, it soon becomes obvious that he is not malicious by nature. He reacts as any human being might, suffering when he is cold, and enjoying warmth and comfort. He feels joy and sorrow.

In *Frankenstein*, emotions are responsible for many of the characters' actions. An important characteristic of the Romantic movement was the emphasis placed on emotion and intuition. Emotions were employed in the creation of art; in her characterization of the creature, Shelley describes the "monster" as a sensitive being, capable of feeling every human emotion. The creature tells Victor he loves virtue, good feeling, and gentle manners, sharply contradicting Frankenstein's notion that the creature is a "monster" and a "demon." Another Romantic notion, seen here, is the idea that humans are born as kindhearted, moral beings. The creature, born a virtuous innocent, is forced to commit evil because of humankind's attitudes, beginning with Victor's rejection of him. The creature's experience is pitiable. He has no idea who he is or how he came to be. Utterly alone, he yearns to be with humans, but suffers with the knowledge that he will never be allowed to join their community and enjoy its warmth and companionship. Although he is unique, he nevertheless is capable of experiencing human pain and emotion, but he is not able to share his feelings or enjoy the healing comfort of other beings. Yet his first reaction to this awareness is not bitterness. He finds a certain degree of contentment in merely observing his adopted human family. Ironically, the creature's loving, unselfish attitude reveals him to be superior to Victor Frankenstein. According to Harold Bloom, "the greatest paradox and most astonishing achievement of Mary Shelley's novel is that the monster is more human than his creator." (Bloom, 4)

Study Questions

1. What is the first food the creature eats when he goes into the forest?

2. What does the creature call the moon?

3. What weapons do the villagers use to attack the creature?

4. What does Agatha, the young girl, do after she finishes playing her musical instrument?

5. Why is the creature perplexed at first by the unhappiness of the peasant family?

6. Who is the saddest member of the peasant family?

7. Do Felix, Agatha, and their father realize it is the creature who is helping them?

8. How does Felix change when Safie arrives?

9. What pet name does Felix call his fiancée?

10. What book does Felix use to instruct Safie?

Answers

1. The creature eats berries he finds growing on a tree.

2. The creature calls the moon the "orb of night."

3. They use stones and "other kinds of missile weapons."

4. Agatha holds her brother and sobs.

5. The family appears to have everything they need—food, shelter, clothing—and the creature doesn't understand that they are actually living in poverty.

6. The creature believes Felix must have suffered more than the others because he appears to be the saddest person in the cottage.

7. They think it is a magical "good spirit" that is helping them.

8. Felix is delighted to see her, and "every trait of sorrow vanished from his face."

9. Felix calls her his "sweet Arabian."

10. Felix reads Volney's *Ruins of Empires*. By listening to Felix read, the creature gains an insight into the "manners, governments, and religions of the different nations of the earth." After hearing about the wonderful and terrible deeds of humankind, the creature wonders how humans could be "at once so powerful, so virtuous, and magnificent, yet so vicious and base."

Suggested Essay Topics

1. Describe the creature's feelings towards Victor when he first came to life. How do they differ from Victor's first reaction to his creation?

2. Discuss the creature's attitude towards knowledge. Why does learning new things excite him and at the same time cause him so much pain?

3. Explain how the creature feels towards the peasant family. Why do you think he is so moved by their gentleness and kindness?

Volume Two: Chapters Six, Seven, Eight, and Nine

New Character:

Safie's father: *a Turkish man Felix helps escape from prison*

Summary

The creature continues his story. After spending months observing the peasant family, he was able to learn their language and their family history. The family, known as the De Laceys, were of noble birth and had lived in France for many years. Safie's father, a Turkish merchant, was on trial for an unknown reason, although political motives were suspected. At the conclusion of the trial, Safie's father was sentenced to death, an obvious injustice, and all Paris was indignant. It was generally considered that the man's religion and wealth, and not the alleged crime, had been the cause of his condemnation.

Felix was aware of the trial, too, and he became angry at the injustice of the proceedings. He offered his assistance to Safie's father and one day, while he was visiting him, he met Safie and they fell in love. When Safie's father became aware of the young man's feelings for his daughter, he offered Felix her hand in marriage in exchange for Felix's help in escaping from prison. Felix could not accept such an indelicate offer, but he continued with his plans for Safie's father's escape. Felix then received several letters from Safie, thanking him for helping her father. She also told him about her mother, a Christian Arab who had been enslaved by the Turks because of her beauty. She won the heart of Safie's father, who married her. As Safie grew up, her mother instructed her in the tenets of the Christian religion, and taught her to aspire to the higher powers of intellect and independence. These ambitions, however, were forbidden to women by Safie's husband's religion. But Safie longed to marry a Christian and live in a country where women were allowed to "take a rank" in society.

After the escape, Felix left the country with Safie and her father. The government, however, suspected the De Lacey family of helping the Turkish merchant. Agatha and her father were thrown into prison for five months. Felix returned to France, but he could not help his family. After their trial, the De Laceys lost their fortune and were banished from France, eventually moving to Germany. Safie's father betrayed Felix and returned to Turkey, intending to take his daughter with him. But Safie refused to abandon Felix and she eventually followed him to Germany. The creature tells Victor that he was impressed by the De Laceys' story and very moved by their spirit of "benevolence and generosity."

The creature says he remained in the shed, happy to be close to a family like the De Laceys. One night, while looking for food, he found a "leathern portmanteau" that contained several articles of clothing, and some books, including works by Milton, Goethe, and Plutarch. From Plutarch's *Lives* he learned the histories of the first founders of the ancient republics, and the value of "high thoughts." From the *Sorrows* of Werter, the creature comes to understand "despondency and gloom." The books stimulated him emotionally and intellectually, and he was moved and fascinated when he read about the creation of man in Milton's *Paradise Lost*. The creature tells Victor he knows he was rejected by his creator, the way Satan was; and he also understands that, like Adam, he is alone and has no mate. Adam, however, had come forth "from the hands of God a perfect creature, happy and prosperous, guarded by the especial care of his Creator; he was allowed to converse with, and acquire knowledge from beings of a superior nature." Unlike Adam, the creature says he is "wretched, helpless, and alone." This is why he often considered Satan a "fitter emblem" of his condition. And when he saw the happiness of others, "the bitter gall of envy" rose within him.

He goes on to tell Victor that one day, while he was living in the De Laceys' shed, he happened to discover Frankenstein's journal in one of the pockets of the cloak he had taken from Victor's laboratory. After he learned to read, he studied the journal and read about Victor's experiment and discovered how he was created. He also came to understand that it was Victor Frankenstein, his creator, who had abandoned him.

After this discovery, the creature compared the De Laceys' loving care for each other to Frankenstein's behavior towards his own creation. He cursed Frankenstein in a rage, but sought the kindness

of the elder De Lacey, who was blind. Desperate to speak to him, the creature waited until the young people left the cottage. The creature entered the cottage and engaged old De Lacey in conversation. He told De Lacey that he was alone and had "no relation or friend upon earth." The old man agreed that it is a terrible thing to be alone, but urged him not to despair. "To be friendless is indeed to be unfortunate; but the hearts of men, when unprejudiced by an obvious self-interest, are full of brotherly love and charity." Then he offered the creature his help, telling him "it will afford me true pleasure to be in any way serviceable to a human creature." The creature says he was greatly heartened by the old man's offer, and was about to tell him his story, when Felix and the others returned. Thinking a monster was attacking his father, Felix rushed to defend the old man. He pummeled the creature and threw him out of the cottage. Saddened and hurt by Felix's actions, the creature says he didn't even try to defend himself.

Later, the creature returned to his hiding place in the De Laceys' shed. He waited for them to arise, but soon realized their cottage was empty. In the morning, Felix returned with another man and the creature listened as Felix told the man his family was terrified and could never live in the cottage again. The creature sinks into a state of "utter and stupid despair," and for the first time he experienced the feelings of "revenge and hatred." Later that night, he burned the cottage down, dancing around it "with fury." The creature says he continued to roam through the forest, in "agony," although when spring arrived, he briefly felt the joy and spirit of the season. For a moment, he "dared to be happy." Then, as he continued through the woods, he saw a young girl slip and fall into a stream. The creature pulled her from the water; she was unconscious and he attempted to revive her. However, a man emerged from the woods and shot the creature, wounding him, then grabbed the girl and ran off. Once again, the creature was enraged; his kind act had only resulted in his own pain and misery. His gentle feelings gave way to "hellish rage" and he vowed "eternal hatred and vengeance to all mankind."

The creature curses Frankenstein, recalling the sad event and says from that day, he "declared an everlasting war against the species" and against "him who had formed me." All his former feelings of kindness turned to hatred and a desire for revenge. After he recovered from his gunshot wound, he roamed for months, searching for Victor, and finally made his way to Geneva. There he saw a beautiful young boy with whom he tried to make friends. He thought that the boy would be too young to have formed any prejudices and decided to seize him in order to "educate him as his companion and friend." But the boy was horrified by the creature's appearance. When the creature learned that the boy's name was Frankenstein, he killed him in a rage and took his locket. The creature tells Victor "I gazed on my victim, and my heart swelled with exultation and hellish triumph." He now understood that he, too, was capable of creating death and despair. He knew that this was a way to get revenge on his creator. Later he found a young woman, Justine, sleeping in a barn and he placed William's locket in her apron pocket, thinking she would be blamed for the murder.

The creature laments that now he is alone and in torment. He demands that Frankenstein create another creature, as ugly as he is, so that he can have a companion who won't reject him.

Victor is astounded by the creature's request. At first he refuses; he is furious at the creature for killing William and, indirectly, Justine. Victor also can't bear the thought of being responsible for another horrible monster. But the creature reasons with him. He says he is not evil, only lonely, and therefore miserable. If he had a companion, he would not act with malice towards anyone. If Victor refuses, however, he promises to get revenge so terrible that Victor will "curse the hour of (his) birth." Then he begs Victor to make him happy by granting his demand.

Victor is moved and feels compassion for the creature. He finally agrees to do what the creature asks, but Victor makes him swear to leave Europe and "every other place in the neighborhood of man." The creature agrees, promising to stay away from humans forever if Victor will create a companion for him. He tells Victor to get started on his new creation, promising that he'll be watching. Then he leaves, and Victor, filled with despair about what he has agreed to do, hikes down the mountain to Chamonix where his family had been anxiously waiting the whole night for him to return. When they see him they are alarmed by his haggard appearance. The following day the family returns to Geneva.

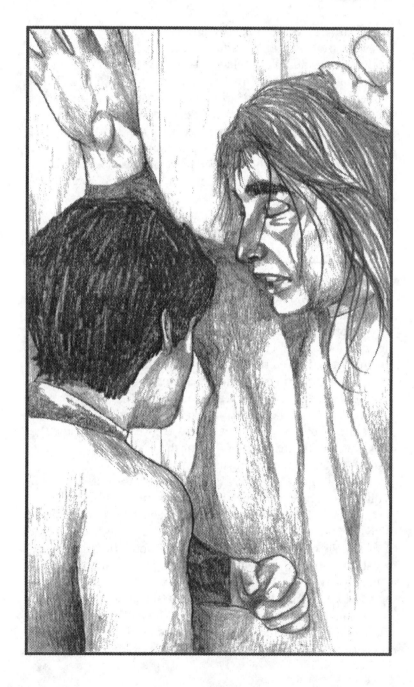

Analysis

The creature exemplifies the Romantic notion that good nature and kindness are inherent qualities in human beings. Evil results only after the harsh actions of society have taken their toll. The creature is benign, and eager for love and compassion, when he is first created. He responds strongly to the love the De Laceys have for each other, and to Felix's obvious sadness. He is happy when Safie visits and Felix's mood improves. Again, the contrast to Victor's description of the evil, malicious creature is striking.

When he was created, the creature was deformed, but he wasn't a monster. His murderous actions may have turned him into a demon, but only after he was repeatedly abused and rejected by humans. Even after being abandoned by Victor and assaulted by Felix, the creature finds it in his heart to help a human when he saves the drowning girl. But once again, his reward is abuse when the girl's father tries to kill him. Young William's rejection is the final blow. When the boy reveals that his name is Frankenstein, the creature loses control. He performs a horrible act by murdering a child. The creature is exultant after he commits the crime, but only after suffering the cruelty and prejudice of humankind that leads to his desire for revenge. The evil is a product of society's cold rejection of the creature.

When the creature reads Milton's *Paradise Lost*, he finds many parallels to his own existence. He even calls the book a "true history." He sees himself as a being created by a God who is at war with his own creations. John Milton's *Paradise Lost* was written in 1667. The entire work, a poem divided into 12 books, tells the story of the temptation and fall of Adam and Eve. The poem describes Satan's expulsion from heaven, the war of the angels, and the creation of hell and Satan's offspring, Death and Sin. Milton also offers the promise of salvation by a "greater man," or Jesus Christ. At the conclusion of the poem, Adam and Eve are forced to leave Paradise. The creature identifies with Adam, who, when created, was completely alone, and whose happy innocence was lost; but he also compares himself to Satan, the fallen angel. The creature suffers terribly, tormented by the knowledge that the love and kindness that exist in the world will never be available to him. Frankenstein, his creator, is the creature's God, and only Frankenstein has the

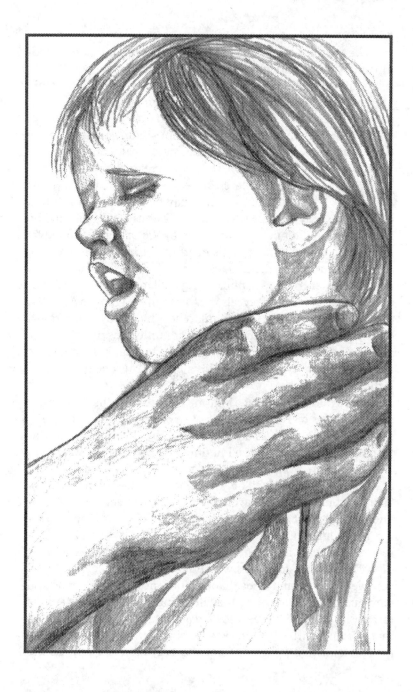

knowledge and power to give life to another being. The creature's existence, however, is hardly a blessing and he considers Frankenstein to have cursed him by bringing him to life."

Study Questions

1. What French city did the De Laceys live in?

2. At the conclusion of his trial, what sentence does Safie's father receive?

3. Why didn't Safie's father want her to marry Felix?

4. What does Safie take with her when she leaves Turkey?

5. What are the creature's "chief delights" when he is living in the shed?

6. How does old De Lacey describe the hearts of men to the creature?

7. What does the De Lacey family do after their encounter with the creature?

8. What does the creature do to the De Laceys' cottage?

9. What happens when the creature sees the young girl fall into the stream?

10. Why does the creature think William will not be frightened by his appearance?

Answers

1. The De Laceys lived in Paris.

2. Safie's father is condemned to death.

3. He loathed the idea that she would ever marry a Christian.

4. Safie takes her jewels and a small sum of money.

5. The creature enjoys nature, especially in the summer, delighting in "the sight of the flowers, the birds, and all the gay apparel."

6. He says the hearts of men, when unprejudiced by self-interest, are "full of brotherly love and charity."

7. They move out of the cottage and the creature never sees them again.

8. The creature burns it to the ground.

9. The creature saves her from drowning and pulls her back to safety.

10. When the creature meets William, whom he at first only knows as an anonymous boy, he believes the boy is too young to have formed any prejudices about "deformity." The creature mistakenly thinks the boy will accept the way he looks.

Suggested Essay Topics

1. Discuss the Romantic notion of good and evil. How does it relate to the creature's actions so far?

2. Explain why the creature feels it is so important to come out of hiding and talk to the elder De Lacey.

3. Describe how the creature feels when he finds Victor's journal in his pocket.

Volume Three: Chapters One and Two

Summary

After his return to Geneva, Victor finds that he is unable to "collect the courage" to begin work on the creature's companion. He cannot overcome his repugnance to the work he must do, and he knows he will have to devote several months to the project. Victor tells us that he "clung to every pretense of delay, and could not resolve to interrupt my returning tranquility." But he realizes that, eventually, he will have to begin the dreaded task and fulfill his promise to the creature.

Alphonse is worried about Victor because he seems so depressed. He suggests that Victor and Elizabeth marry, hoping they will find happiness together. Although he loves Elizabeth, Victor cannot imagine getting married in light of the awful thing he has agreed to do for the creature. He assures his father that he will eventually marry Elizabeth, but he cannot tell him the reason he must wait. Alphonse then arranges for Victor to go to England with Henry Clerval to study. He hopes that the "amusement of traveling" will help restore Victor's tranquility. Elizabeth is sad that Victor is leaving, but she hopes he will return a happier person. She regrets that she does not have the same opportunities "of enlarging her experience."

Victor sets off on his trip and meets Clerval in Strasbourg and together they set off for London. They travel along the Rhine from Strasbourg to Rotterdam, where they plan to take a ship to England. On their voyage down the Rhine they pass many beautiful towns and islands, traveling through Mannheim and Mayence. Victor describes the picturesque hills, castles, and vineyards they see along the banks. Throughout the trip, Clerval is anxious to arrive in London and eager to meet new people, but Victor remains sad and unenthusiastic. Clerval realizes that his friend is depressed. As they travel, he points out the beauty of the landscape, telling Victor, "This is what it is to live; now I enjoy existence!" But Victor can only brood, thinking of himself as a "miserable wretch, haunted by a curse that shut up every avenue to enjoyment." He knows that soon he will have to begin work on the new creature.

After living in London for several months, Victor and Henry travel north to Scotland. Along the way, Victor is convinced that the creature is following him. A week after their arrival in Edinburgh, Victor tells Henry that he wants to work alone for a while. Victor fears that the creature will be getting impatient; he fears for the safety of his family, and he knows he must begin his work immediately.

Victor travels to a remote island in Scotland and rents a "miserable hut," where he intends to finish his dreaded task. However, he finds it very difficult to work, having none of the enthusiasm he had when he first began his work in Ingolstadt. He fears meeting the creature again, and he constantly questions himself because he feels sick and filled with "forebodings of evil" about what he is doing.

Analysis

Although he is the same age as Clerval, Victor seems much older. The dreadful experiences he has had since he left the

university have weighted him down with worry and despair. He no longer shares Clerval's intellectual curiosity and excitement; his life is filled with fear and regret. The enthusiasm and ambition he had only a few years earlier have now led him to a barren island where he must complete a dreaded task. Now when he describes himself he says, "I am a blasted tree; the bolt has entered my soul...." This is an image that recalls the giant oak Victor saw destroyed by lightning when he was 15. That event, which so excited him then, inspired him to the scientific explorations that took him to Ingolstadt and resulted in his creating a monster. It is an ironic comment on Victor's youthful quest, an ambitious pursuit filled with hope and promise that has now resulted in Victor's present state of loathing and misery.

As Victor travels with Clerval, the only pleasure he takes is in the magnificent scenery, finding solace there as he did in the natural surroundings of the Alps. Travel through wild, rugged terrain not only inspires Victor, but it also gives him a chance to be alone with his thoughts. Scotland, the Alps, and the Rhine were favorite locations for a number of Romantic writers. The importance of these settings becomes apparent when, in spite of his awful situation, Victor takes time in his narrative to describe some of the sights he and Clerval visit along the Rhine, and in England and Scotland. "Even I," he says, as they sail down the Rhine, "depressed in mind, and my spirits continually agitated by gloomy feelings, even I was pleased." Later, again in typical Romantic fashion, Victor isolates himself, not only to set up a new laboratory, but also to wrestle with his personal demons. He chooses a remote, barren island as the place to begin work on the new creature, a place surrounded by wild seas and jagged, rocky cliffs.

Shelley establishes the mood of each scene through the actions and emotions of her characters, and by choosing dramatic settings. By placing Victor on the Scottish island, she uses the Romantic device of employing remote, exotic locations to set a mood, as well as to provide a contrast to Victor's psychological and emotional pain. It is also a frightening place, adding to the suspense of the story. Typically, these exotic locales were used by Romantic writers to provide an exciting, intriguing locale for their characters to find solace, or to seek adventure. But Victor knows that an awful job is waiting for him when he reaches the island. Instead of finding comfort, alone, in this desolate place, Victor knows he is being watched. He grows increasingly "restless and nervous," a feeling compounded by "a solitude where nothing could for an instant call my attention from the actual scene in which I was engaged."

Study Questions

1. Why does Victor want to go to England?

2. Why does Alphonse want Victor to marry Elizabeth?

3. How long does Victor plan to be away from Geneva?

4. What does Victor take with him on his trip?

5. What poem does Victor quote from as he describes the beautiful scenery on his trip?

6. In London, why does Clerval remind Victor of his "former self"?

7. Why does Victor agree to go to Scotland?

8. How does Victor feel when he and Henry visit Hampden's tomb?

9. While he is traveling in Scotland, what does Victor fear the creature might do?

10. To what islands does Victor travel in Scotland?

Answers

1. He wants to go to England to create a companion for the creature; Victor must continue his studies and learn about the new scientific discoveries that were made in England.

2. Alphonse realizes that his son is depressed; he hopes the marriage will make him happy.

3. Victor plans to be away for two years.

4. At the last minute, Victor remembers to pack his chemical instruments.

5. Victor quotes from Wordsworth's "Tintern Abbey."

6. Victor says Clerval is "inquisitive, and anxious to gain experience and instruction." He reminds Victor of himself when he was young and enthusiastic.

7. Although he "abhorred society" and doesn't want to visit any new friends, Victor is anxious to see mountains and streams again, and to be in a natural setting.

8. For a moment, Victor forgets his troubles. He feels free, filled with a "lofty spirit" as he recalls Hampden's heroic deeds.

9. Victor is afraid the creature will kill his family in Geneva, although he also thinks the creature is following him.

10. Victor goes to the Orkney Islands to begin working on the companion for the creature.

Suggested Essay Topics

1. Victor says of his father that "a more indulgent and less dictatorial parent did not exist upon earth." Discuss Alphonse's influence on Victor and Victor's feelings towards his father.

2. Give some examples of the Romantic concept in Shelley's use of physical locations. How does it help establish character and mood in the novel?

Volume Three: Chapters Three and Four

New Characters:

Mr. Kirwin: *a judicial magistrate who is in charge of Victor's case in Ireland*

Daniel Nugent: *a witness in the murder case in Ireland*

Nurse: *a woman who cares for Victor in prison*

Summary

As he labors to bring life to the new creature, Victor recalls his earlier efforts, three years ago in Ingolstadt. He was full of hope then, excited about his experiment, but the result had been a disaster, filling his heart with "the bitterest remorse." Now, as he works in his makeshift laboratory, Victor begins to worry about what will happen when he brings the new creature to life. What if this creature, a female, refuses to abide by the terms of the agreement he made with the first creature? She could be just as angry as the male, and feel as alienated by her deformed appearance. Or, what if she doesn't like the first creature? What would happen if they hate each other? And suppose she is as evil and vengeful as the first creature? Then another horrifying thought consumes Victor when he wonders if the creatures will mate, starting a new, terrible race of beings.

As Victor considers these gruesome possibilities, the creature appears, peering in at him through a window. Shocked at the sight of him, Victor instantly realizes that he cannot keep his promise. As the creature watches, he destroys his new creation, tearing it apart. Outside, the creature lets out an anguished howl and runs off into the night. Later, the creature returns and tells Victor that he is suffering terribly because of what Victor has done. Now he knows he will be alone, without hope, forever. Again, he demands that Victor do as he asks and make him a companion. But Victor is defiant and unafraid. The creature calls Victor his "slave" and reminds him that he has power over him. He tells Victor, "I can make you so wretched that the light of day will be hateful to you. You are my creator, but I am your master;—obey!" But Victor tells him that his threats "cannot move me to do an act of wickedness." They only confirm his decision to not create another monster. The creature asks why, if every living man and beast has a mate, he should be alone? "I had feelings of affection," the creature says, "but they were requited by detestation and scorn." The creature vows revenge; he vows that Victor will live to "curse the sun that gazes on your misery." Then the creature tells Victor that he will be with him on his wedding night. Victor lunges at him, but the creature escapes.

After the creature departs, Victor leaves his cottage and walks on the beach. He encounters some fishermen who have a packet of letters for him. One letter is from Henry Clerval, suggesting that they meet in Perth and travel to France together. Victor says this letter "recalled me to life." He decides to leave the island in two days. Victor returns to his laboratory to clean up the remains of the second creature. He looks at the half-finished creature, feeling as if he had "mangled the living flesh of a human being." Victor gathers his laboratory instruments and sinks them into the sea. Then, in the middle of the night, Victor takes the remains of the unfinished creature and throws them into the sea. As he disposes of the female he thinks of the first creature's threat. He feels he is doing the right thing, but nevertheless, he is haunted by his own actions.

Victor then falls asleep in his boat; caught in a strong wind, he drifts far out to sea. When he awakens he is sailing towards Ireland. As Victor comes ashore, he is confronted by an angry crowd. Before Victor can explain himself, the crowd takes him before the local magistrate, Mr. Kirwin. There, Victor is shocked to learn that a man was murdered the night before in a local village. A witness testifies that the man had been strangled. The crowd has brought Victor before the magistrate because they suspect him of committing the murder.

A number of witnesses testify before Mr. Kirwin. Victor listens as they describe finding the body of a man on the beach. The man had apparently been strangled, for the witnesses describe black finger marks on his neck. When Victor hears this, he recalls the death of his brother, William, who had the same finger marks on his neck, and becomes extremely agitated. His limbs tremble and he fights to hold back tears. The magistrate observes Victor's reaction and draws an unfavorable conclusion. When the witnesses finish, Victor is taken to see the corpse of the strangled man. He looks at the body and is horrified to see that it is his dear friend, Henry Clerval. He cries out, "Have my murderous machinations deprived you also, my dearest Henry, of life? Two I have already destroyed; other victims await their destiny: but you, Clerval, my friend, my benefactor—" Then Victor collapses and is carried from the room. He remains in a delirious state for almost two months, and when he is finally lucid again, he realizes that he is in prison. Victor learns that he has been charged with the murder and will remain in prison until his trial.

As Victor begins to recover from his illness, he becomes better acquainted with the magistrate, Mr. Kirwin. Although Victor must remain in prison, Mr. Kirwin treats him kindly, giving Victor the best room in the dingy place, and sending a doctor and nurse to

attend to him. Victor appreciates Kirwin's attention, but he tells him, "on the whole earth there is no comfort which I am capable of receiving." Kirwin, however, continues to express great concern about Victor's situation. He tells Victor he wrote to his father and Victor is immediately worried about the welfare of his family, fearing the creature may have harmed them. But Kirwin assures Victor that his family is well, and tells him his father has come to see him. When Alphonse arrives, Victor is overjoyed to see him. Alphonse assures Victor that the family is well, but laments his son's latest misfortune. When Victor's case is brought before the grand jury, it is rejected; there is evidence proving that Victor was on the Orkney Islands at the time of the murder. Alphonse is relieved when his son is freed, but Victor remains despondent. He feels that his life has been ruined forever. All he can think of is his murdered friend, Henry, and the "watery, clouded eyes of the monster." As Victor leaves the prison, a free man, he overhears someone remark that he may be innocent of murder, but it is obvious that he has a guilty conscience about something else. Then Victor and Alphonse travel to Dublin where they board a ship to begin their journey back to Geneva. On the voyage home, Victor has a frightful dream, remembering the quiet happiness of his life in Geneva, the death of his mother, and his departure for Ingolstadt. In his dream, he recalls the "mad enthusiasm" that led to his creating the monster, his "hideous enemy," and the night he was brought to life. After a restless sleep, as he is waking up, Victor imagines the creature's hands around his neck.

Analysis

When Victor agrees to create the female creature, he immediately regrets making the promise, but he is afraid of what the monster might do if he refuses the demand. Now, a greater worry for Victor is the thought that the second creature will be as evil as the original, or worse. He fears he will unleash a brutal horror upon an unsuspecting world. This is a chance he cannot take, and a responsibility he is unwilling to bear. After he created the first creature, Victor was reluctant to tell anyone about his bizarre experiment. When the creature kills William, Victor allows Justine to be hanged for the crime. Later, he goes to England, thinking the creature may strike again, yet he warns no one about it. As he works on the second creature though, the full weight of responsibility is upon him. He can no longer deny what he has done, nor can he fulfill his gruesome promise to the monster he created.

As he destroys the half-finished creature, Victor commits the ultimate act of human cruelty against his living creation. In front of him, he tears the companion to pieces, condemning the original creature to a wretched, lonely existence without a mate. The creature, who began life innocently, eager for love and understanding, now tells Victor that his only remaining passion is his desire for revenge. In destroying his potential mate, Frankenstein has crushed his last hope. "You can blast my other passions," the creature says, "but revenge remains—revenge, henceforth dearer than light or food!" However, Victor has finally accepted responsibility for the havoc he created when he brought his creature to life. He knows he will have to endure the creature's wrath and suffer the consequences of his actions.

The irony of Henry Clerval's death is apparent to Victor. Earlier he had described his friend as eager and full of life. Victor, of course, was half-dead and filled with despair. Now, Henry is dead and Victor lives, and the creature has murdered another innocent person to satisfy his vow of revenge. One by one, the creature is eliminating loved ones from Victor's life. Victor is plagued by misery and regret. He believes he has destroyed not only his own life, but also the lives of his young brother, an innocent young woman, and his closest friend.

Victor began to cut himself off from his friends and family when he went to Ingolstadt. Obsessed with his studies and experiments, he became remote, growing distant and strange. The existence of the creature served to further isolate him. He wouldn't tell anyone what he had done and he was filled with dread and despair. The creature understands this and he chooses not to kill Victor; instead, he methodically eliminates love and companionship from Victor's life. Now Victor, the creator, will know, as his creature does, the torment of loneliness and seclusion.

Study Questions

1. Where does the creature go after Frankenstein destroys the female creature?

2. What do the fishermen deliver to Victor while he is sitting on the beach?

3. Does Victor ever reconsider his actions after he destroys the female creature?

4. Is Victor afraid when he is adrift at sea?

5. What language does Victor use to address the Irish people?

6. How does Victor describe Mr. Kirwin?

7. What did the fishermen do when they found Clerval's body?

8. While he is delirious, what does Victor say that implicates him in the murder of Clerval?

9. What does the prison nurse tell Victor about his father?

10. Does Victor care that he is in prison?

Answers

1. The creature runs out of Frankenstein's hut and rows out to sea.

2. The fishermen deliver a letter from Clerval suggesting that they travel to France together.

3. After he destroys the creature, Victor doubts himself, wondering if he did the right thing. But he says, "I banished from my mind every thought that could lead to a different conclusion."

4. Even though he is miserable, Victor is grateful to be alive when the sea becomes calm and he sees land in the distance.

5. Victor speaks to them in English.

6. Mr. Kirwin is an "old, benevolent man, with calm and mild manners."

7. The fishermen brought the body to a nearby house and went to town for a doctor.

8. Victor blames himself for the deaths of Henry, William, and Justine, raving that he is the murderer of all three.

9. She tells him that his father has come to visit him.

10. Because he is in such anguish, it makes no difference to him. Victor tells us that "to me the walls of a dungeon or a palace were alike hateful."

Suggested Essay Topics

1. Discuss Victor's reluctance to create the second creature. Why do you think he destroys it in front of the other creature?

2. What does the creature mean when he tells Victor, "I shall be with you on your wedding night"?

3. Compare Alphonse's and Victor's relationship to Victor's relationship with the creature.

Volume Three: Chapters Five and Six

New Characters:

Magistrate: *a criminal judge in Geneva who listens to Victor's story about the creature*

Summary

Victor continues to blame himself for the deaths of William, Justine, and Henry. He says, "I am the assassin of those most innocent victims; they died by my machinations." Because he created the creature and unleashed it on the world, he feels that he is really their killer and, therefore, is unfit to live among other human beings. During his imprisonment, Alphonse had often heard Victor make the assertion that he was responsible for the deaths, but he can't understand why Victor feels this way. He wonders if his son is mad.

Victor and Alphonse leave Ireland and travel to France; while they are in Paris, Victor receives a letter from Elizabeth. She tells him that he is free from any obligation of marriage. Elizabeth says she realizes that, in the course of his travels, Victor may have found someone else. However, Victor still loves Elizabeth and he decides to go ahead with the marriage, hoping it will at least make her and Alphonse happy. But Victor can't forget the creature's threat that he will be with him on his wedding night. He writes back to Elizabeth and tells her that he has a dreadful secret he will reveal upon his return to Geneva.

When Victor and Alphonse return home, Elizabeth is disturbed by Victor's emaciated appearance. Elizabeth has also changed, thinner now, and no longer a vivacious beauty. They go ahead with their wedding plans, in spite of Victor's fears that the monster will arrive and make good on his threat. Alphonse arranges for Elizabeth to recover part of her inheritance—a villa, which will be the couple's honeymoon suite. Before the wedding, Victor arms himself with daggers and pistols in case the monster attacks him. Victor assumes the creature will try to murder him. After the ceremony, Victor and Elizabeth sail to Evian where they plan to spend the night at an inn. As the sun sets, Victor is filled with apprehension, wondering if the monster will appear.

That night, a vicious thunderstorm makes Victor even more worried. Leaving Elizabeth in their room, Victor roams through the inn, checking the rooms and hallways to make sure they are secure. Suddenly, he hears a scream and he rushes back to the bedroom where he finds Elizabeth, strangled to death on the bed. Victor faints, but when he comes to a moment later, he sees the monster grinning at him through the window and pointing to the body of Elizabeth. The monster runs off as Victor fires his pistol at him. Other guests join Victor in the pursuit, but the monster has disappeared.

Victor, terribly distraught, is carried back to the inn. He can't believe that his wife has been murdered, and now he fears that the monster will go after his father and the rest of his family. Victor knows that it is his own creation that has destroyed his life, his friends, and his family. When he returns to Geneva, his father is alive but he soon becomes gravely ill from grief over the loss of Elizabeth. When he dies, Victor goes mad and is taken to an asylum. Months later, after he is released, Victor appears before a local magistrate. He tells the official about the monster and the deaths of friends and family. Although the magistrate doesn't believe his story, he warns Victor that such a powerful monster could never be caught. Victor, however, is undeterred. He vows revenge against the creature and sets off to find him.

Analysis

The creature has now completed his revenge, infusing Victor with as much hatred for him as the creature feels for mankind. When Victor sets off to seek his own revenge, he is dooming himself to a life of hardship, frustration, and misery. Victor had assumed the creature would try to kill him on his wedding night, but the creature had other plans. He is well aware that death will bring release from the torment of existence. When he murders Elizabeth he is avenging the death of his own "bride"—the creature Victor tore apart in Scotland. But the creature intends to let Victor live, ensuring that his creator will suffer an equal amount of pain and misery.

In her essay, "Bearing Demons: Frankenstein's Circumvention of the Maternal," which is included in *Mary Shelley's Frankenstein* (see bibliography), Margaret Homans argues that the creature had long ago replaced Elizabeth as Victor's chief concern. Frankenstein has devoted an enormous amount of love and attention to his studies, and to the actual creation of the monster. In fact, Victor is so absorbed, he doesn't even notice how ugly the creature is until it comes to life. Although she knows nothing about the creature, Elizabeth even hints at Victor's obsession in her letter, asking him if he still wants to marry her, and wondering if he has met someone else. Elizabeth's murder by the creature, Homans says, "suggests not so much revenge as jealousy." Clearly, the creature resents any attempt Victor makes to be happy; happiness is not available to the creature, and it is Victor who is responsible for the creature's existence. The creature will never allow Victor a moment's joy or peace. Victor's life is now as ruined as his monster's.

Victor finally seeks the help of society when he is alone and desperately in need. But when Victor tells the magistrate his story, the judge refuses to believe him. Again, the monster has triumphed; Victor is abandoned by his community and, like the creature, must go off by himself on a lonely quest for revenge.

Study Questions

1. After he is released from prison, does Victor tell his father about the creature?

2. Why do Victor and Alphonse go to Paris?

3. Besides thinking that Victor may have found someone else, why does Elizabeth believe that Victor may not really want to marry her?

4. Does Elizabeth love Victor?

5. How does Victor behave in the days leading up to his wedding?

6. What does Victor think the monster plans to do on Victor's wedding night?

7. Where do Victor and Elizabeth intend to live after their wedding?

8. How does Victor get back to Geneva from Evian?

9. How does the magistrate react when Victor tells him his story?

10. What is Victor's response to the magistrate?

Answers

1. Even though Alphonse wonders why his son keeps blaming himself for the murders, Victor never tells him about the creature.

2. Alphonse has to attend to some business there.

3. When Elizabeth saw Victor in Geneva, she assumed he was depressed because of his obligation to marry her.

4. She loves him, but she worries that he is not really interested in marrying her.

5. Victor pretends to be happy. He fools his father, but not Elizabeth.

6. Victor thinks the monster will try to kill him.

7. Victor and Elizabeth plan to live in a house that was purchased for them near Cologne.

8. He can't sail because of the storm, so he hires several men to help him row back to Geneva.

9. He is incredulous at first, but he soon grows more interested and shudders with horror as Victor relates his tale.

10. Victor becomes enraged when the magistrate, who doesn't believe him, tries to calm him down.

Suggested Essay Topics

1. Compare the events that occur on Victor's wedding night to the night when Victor destroyed the second creature.

2. Did it surprise you that the creature killed Elizabeth and not Victor? Explain your answer.

3. Why do you think Victor finally tells the magistrate about the creature?

Volume Three: Chapter Seven

Summary

Victor begins his search for the monster. Before he leaves Geneva, he visits the graves of Elizabeth, Alphonse, and William. In the cemetery, he swears that he will find and destroy the creature. As he stands by their graves, he hears a "fiendish laugh"; the monster has followed him to the graveyard. The monster tells Victor he is satisfied that Victor has decided to go on living. He understands that Victor's suffering will continue. Victor chases after the creature, but all he sees is its shape, running with great speed, away from the cemetery.

Since that night, Victor says he has been in constant pursuit of the creature, traveling around the world and enduring terrible hardships. He followed the creature through the frozen lands of Tartary and Russia, exhausted and hungry, eating wild game and depending on the friendship of some villagers who often provided him with shelter and a fire for cooking his meal. During this time, the only thing that kept him going was his single-minded obsession for revenge. At one point, he followed the monster onto a ship that sailed on the Black Sea, but he was unable to catch him. Victor then traveled from village to village, seeking information from local people who may have seen the creature. Victor's only happiness came when he would sleep, dreaming of Elizabeth and Clerval, the "benevolent countenance" of his father, and his "beloved country." He would dream of being in the arms of his friends, and even during the day, he sometimes would persuade himself that they were still alive.

The monster begins leaving Victor messages, hinting at where he is headed. He taunts Victor, writing, "My reign is not yet over, you live, and my power is complete." In another message, the creature tells Victor: "Prepare! Your toils only begin: wrap yourself in furs, and provide food, for we shall soon enter upon a journey where your sufferings will satisfy my everlasting hatred." He informs Victor that he is going north, where the ice and cold, which don't bother him, will make Victor suffer even more. But Victor is not dissuaded and he continues to pursue the creature, outfitting himself with heavy furs and a dogsled team. Another note from the creature has informed him that they are heading into the Arctic. The monster torments Victor by appearing in the distance and then racing away before Victor can catch him. At this point, Victor has become oblivious to the passage of time. He is unaware of how many months have passed since he began chasing the creature. He continues his pursuit over the Arctic ice fields, but as his sled dogs die, he realizes that he may be facing death himself. Stranded on a sheet of ice, unable to travel, Victor was likely to die when he encountered Walton's ship.

Victor tells Walton that he has recovered, thanks to his new friend's kind attention and care. But, Victor says, he must continue to pursue the monster. He can't ask Walton to go with him, of course; the hardships are too great, so he will go on alone. His only fear is that he may die before he completes his task. He begs Walton to kill the monster for him if this happens. Walton now continues the narrative in other letters to his sister.

Letter of August 26, 17—

Walton writes to his sister, Margaret Saville, that Victor's story might be unbelievable except for the fact that he has seen the monster himself. He has also seen the letters of Felix and Safie, and most of all, has heard the anguish of Victor Frankenstein, and his broken voice, and seen his face suddenly change to an "expression of the wildest rage." Therefore, he believes Victor, even though his story is incredible. He tells Margaret that Victor read over the account Walton had written down, making certain corrections to ensure its accuracy. When Walton asked about the creature's appearance, Victor refused to give a complete physical description of the monster. "Are you mad, my friend?" Victor asked Walton. "Would you also create for yourself and the world a demoniacal enemy?" Victor tells him not to ask such questions.

Walton goes on to describe Victor as a great friend, and a man of wit and intelligence. He hopes that he can persuade Victor to give up his quest and learn to enjoy life again. But Victor does not think he will ever be able to live a normal life, and he can't imagine ever recovering from the loss of Elizabeth and Clerval. Now, Victor has told Walton, he lives only for revenge. He says that only when he catches and destroys the monster, his own creation, will he finally be fulfilled and able to die in peace.

Letter of September 2—

Walton writes that his ship continues to be surrounded by enormous mountains of ice. He fears he and his crew all might perish. Victor, who has grown close to Walton, offers him words of hope and tries to reassure him that the ice will break soon. Victor's words are the only thing that make Walton feel better. He says that "even the sailors feel the power of his eloquence."

Letter of September 5—

The ship is still stranded in the ice. Walton's crew has asked him to return home if the ice breaks. They are afraid to go on and Walton agrees, assuring them he will turn the ship around if the ice releases them. Victor, whose health has once again taken a turn for the worse, is shocked that Walton would give up and abandon his "glorious expedition."

Letter of September 7—

A brief note. Walton writes: "The die is cast; I have consented to return, if we are not destroyed." His hopes, he says, have been "blasted by cowardice and indecision."

Letter of September12—

The ice breaks and the ship is ready to return to England. Victor refuses to give up the chase, but when he tries to get out of bed, he collapses. The ship's doctor tells Walton that Victor is going to die. On his death bed, Victor insists that he was right to not create the second monster. The potential for evil was too great, and he had a duty to protect his "fellow creatures" from another monstrous creation. But he now understands that it was his own ambition and selfish dreams that led to the creation of the monster and the tragedies that followed. He urges Walton to seek "happiness in tranquility, and avoid ambition, even if it be only the apparently innocent one of distinguishing yourself in science and discoveries." He goes on to say, "I myself have been blasted in these hopes, yet another may succeed." Now that he knows he will die soon, Victor finally experiences some peace and tranquility himself, no longer feeling the "burning hatred, and ardent desire of revenge." He releases Walton from his obligation to pursue the creature. Then Victor Frankenstein dies with a "gentle smile" on his lips.

Victor's body is placed in a coffin. A while later, Walton hears a noise coming from Victor's room. He rushes in and discovers the monster standing over the coffin, uttering "exclamations of grief and horror." Walton writes that he had never seen a being with such a horrible face of "appalling hideousness." The creature then asks for Victor's forgiveness. He tells Walton that even though he was responsible for Victor's misery, he felt sorry for him. But the creature, too, has suffered terribly. All he wanted was to be accepted by someone who could look past his monstrous appearance and appreciate his inner being. He says he was once filled with "sublime and transcendent visions," but he was "miserable and abandoned" by the human race and couldn't bear living life alone. He never wanted to harm anyone, but his treatment by humans caused him such suffering that all he wanted was revenge. "Think ye that the groans of Clerval were music to my ear? My heart was fashioned to be susceptible of love and sympathy; and, when wrenched by misery to vice and hatred, it did not endure the violence of the change without torture, such as you cannot even imagine." After he murdered Clerval, the creature says he pitied Frankenstein and hated himself. He knew that his "insatiable thirst for vengeance" would only cause him misery, but, he says, "I was the slave, not the master of an impulse, which I detested, yet could not disobey." Now that his revenge is complete, all he desires is death.

The creature tells Walton that he will leave the ship and travel north where he will build a funeral pyre and burn himself to death. He bids farewell to Victor and insists that although Victor suffered terribly, he—the creature—suffered more. Then the creature leaps out the window, onto the floating ice, and is carried away by the waves, "lost in darkness and distance."

Analysis

Even on his death bed, Victor is reluctant to give up the driving ambition that has ultimately brought him to his present state of misery. Although Victor advises Walton to give up his ambition, he also urges him not to abandon his "glorious" expedition, even though the crew is terrified and the ship, hemmed in by ice, is in a desperate situation. Frankenstein would have them continue, no matter what the cost. Ironically, although he is well aware of the circumstances that have led to his own ruin, he is unable to apply them when he advises his new friend. The quest for a grand achievement, which was his own undoing, continues to be an overriding concern. Like Frankenstein, Walton's dreams have brought him face to face with an unpleasant reality. But he seems to have found some meaning in Victor's tragedy. In spite of his friend's exhortations, common sense and caution prevail. Walton refuses to destroy himself or his crew. While he is overly impressed by the sensitive, intelligent Frankenstein—the great friend he has long been in search of—in the end, he won't take his advice.

With Victor's death, the creature has satisfied his desire for revenge. Victor has suffered terribly, both physically and emotionally, and he has endured the gradual destruction of his family, his life, and his future. It is a hollow victory for the creature, though, and he mourns Victor's passing. He still finds it in his heart to feel sorry for his creator, and once his revenge is complete, all he wants to do is die and not leave a trace of himself behind.

Frankenstein was the creator of the creature's body and the manipulator of his emotions. His rejection of the monster results in the vengeful rage that directs the creature's actions during its life. But, in the end, it is the creature who will control his own

action —> reaction

destiny, choosing to die on his terms after destroying Victor. In "Frankenstein's Fallen Angel," an essay in *Mary Shelley's Frankenstein* (see bibliography), Joyce Carol Oates suggests that by the end of the novel, the creature has become "a form of Christ: sinned against by all humankind, yet fundamentally blameless, and yet quite willing to die as a sacrifice." However, because we do not actually witness his death, the possibility arises that, somewhere, he may still exist. He is "a 'modern' species of shadow or Doppelganger," Oates says. "A nightmare that is deliberately created by man's ingenuity and not a mere supernatural being of fairy-tale remnant."

Study Questions

1. As Victor pursues the creature, what is the one thing that gives him pleasure?

2. What clues does the creature leave for Victor?

3. What does the creature steal from the villagers by the sea?

4. Why is Victor stranded on the ice?

5. How does Victor move his ice raft towards Walton's ship?

6. How is the creature's soul described by Victor ?

7. In his youth, what did Victor think he was destined to achieve?

8. Is Margaret Saville married?

9. When Walton's crew wants to return home, what does Victor advise them?

10. Although Frankenstein wanted to destroy the monster, in his speech over Victor's body, what does the creature say would have been a more satisfying revenge?

Answers

1. Victor finds pleasure only when he sleeps at night and dreams of Elizabeth and Henry, alive and healthy.

2. The creature leaves messages carved on rocks and trees.

3. The creature takes their store of winter food and a dogsled team.

4. Victor followed the creature onto the ice and could see him in the distance. But when he is within a mile of him, the creature disappears and the ice breaks apart, leaving Victor stranded.

5. Victor breaks his sled apart and uses the wood to row towards the ship.

6. He says his soul is "as hellish as his form, full of treachery and fiend-like malice."

7. Victor tells Walton that, as a young man, he felt he was destined for "some great enterprise." He believed that his good judgment would enable him to accomplish "illustrious achievements."

8. Yes. Walton mentions that she has a husband and children.

9. Victor tells them not to give into fear and cowardice. They should continue the expedition and return home as heroes.

10. The creature says that Victor's desire for revenge against him would have been "better satiated in my life than in my destruction."

Suggested Essay Topics

1. When Victor is chasing him, why does the creature keep leaving clues to help Victor follow his trail?

2. Do you think Victor is right when he urges Walton to abandon his ambition? Explain your answer.

3. Is Victor justified in blaming himself for the deaths of Henry, Elizabeth, and his other family members? Explain your answer.

4. Discuss the creature's final speech to Walton. How does he really feel about Victor? Is he sad or happy about his death?

5. Why do you think the creature wants to eliminate any evidence of his own existence?

Sample Analytical Paper Topics

Topic #1

Discuss the true nature and personality of the creature in Shelley's *Frankenstein.*

Outline

I. Thesis Statement: *Although the creature behaves viciously and murders several people, he is not inherently evil or malicious.*

II. Creation of the creature

   A. The creature as a product of Victor Frankenstein:

   1. Construction of creature from body parts

   2. Victor brings the creature to life

   3. Rejection of the creature by Frankenstein

   4. Confusion and pain of rejection

   5. Experience of physical senses

   6. Emotional response

   B. The creature as a lost innocent:

   1. Wanders in the woods, alone and confused

   2. Discovery of food and fire

   3. Seeking shelter from natural elements

III. The creature in society

    A. Second rejection by humans:

        1. The peasant flees from the creature

        2. He is isolated from society

    B. Creature understands he is repulsive to humans:

        1. Prefers to hide in the forest, away from people

        2. The creature realizes he is ugly

    C. The benevolent nature of the creature:

        1. Admiration of the De Lacey family

        2. Anonymous acts of kindness towards the family

        3. Appreciation of music and literature

        4. Attempt to communicate with M. De Lacey

            a. Seeks companionship from the father

            b. Experiences sadness instead of anger at Felix's attack

        5. Burns down cottage after De Laceys move out

            a. First violent act in response to rejection

    D. The creature attempts to save the drowning girl:

        1. Attacked by girl's father

        2. Further rejection by society

IV. Creature's relationship with Frankenstein

    A. Rejection and abandonment by "father":

    B. Creature discovers identity of his creator:

        1. Creature experiences true rage

    C. Creature demands a mate from Frankenstein:

        1. Only wants to be left alone with a companion

        2. Promises not to harm anyone

    D. Creature's last hope destroyed by his creator:

    1. Frankenstein tears apart the mate

    2. Creature vows revenge

    3. Kills Henry and Elizabeth

  E. Frankenstein becomes as miserable as his creature:

    1. His loved ones are dead

    2. He feels responsible and guilty over their deaths

V. The creature's true nature and desires

  A. Love and acceptance by society

  B. Companionship

  C. An end to his lonely isolation

  D. Final desire: a fiery, anonymous death;

    1. Creature understands he can never find peace or happiness in human society

  E. The creature as a product of society:

    1. Prejudice and behavior of humans

VI. Conclusion

Topic #2

Illustrate Mary Shelley's use of Romantic concepts in *Frankenstein*.

Outline

I. Thesis Statement: Frankenstein *is a classic example of literature written in the Romantic tradition.*

II. Romanticism

  A. History of romanticism in literature and the arts:

    1. Examples

  B. Characteristics of Romantic literature:

    1. Feelings and emotionalism vs. intellect

    2. Emotional response of characters

    3. Nonrealistic portrayal of characters

    4. Dramatic settings

       a. Mountain landscapes

       b. Germany and the Rhine

       c. Scotland

    5. Bizarre stories and events

  C. Major Romantic writers:

    1. Mary Shelley

    2. Percy Bysshe Shelley

    3. Lord George Gordon Byron

    4. William Wordsworth and Samuel Taylor Coleridge

    5. Sir Walter Scott and Jane Austen

    6. Edgar Allan Poe and the American movement

III. Romantic elements in *Frankenstein*

  A. Bizarre story of monster and creation:

    1. Unexplained events

    2. Strange creature

  B. Characters driven by emotional need:

    1. Creature

       a. Need for love and acceptance

       b. Loneliness and desire for revenge

    2. Victor Frankenstein

       a. Love of friends and family

       b. Despair and shock

       c. Revenge against creature

    3. Elizabeth Lavenza

       a. Love of Victor and family

       b. Belief in Justine's innocence

       c. Self-sacrifice for Victor

     4. Robert Walton

         a. Desire for close, loving friend

     5. Henry Clerval

         a. Close, loyal friend and companion

  C. Romantic settings:

     1. Switzerland and the Alps

     2. Ingolstadt

     3. Scotland and Orkney Islands

     4. The Arctic

  D. Emotional events:

     1. Death of Caroline Beaufort

     2. Adoption of children by Frankensteins

     3. Death of William Frankenstein

     4. Trial of Justine Moritz

     5. Death of Henry Clerval

     6. Marriage of Victor and Elizabeth

     7. Murder of Elizabeth

     8. Death of Victor Frankenstein

  E. Creature as a natural man

     1. Idea of the "Noble Savage"

IV. Conclusion

Topic #3

Victor's driving, obsessive ambition ruined his life and led to his own death and the murder of his loved ones. Illustrate how ambition affects not only Victor and Robert Walton, but also the creature in *Frankenstein.*

Outline

I. Thesis Statement: *Ambition and the quest for knowledge is a fatal flaw in the characters of Victor Frankenstein, Robert Walton, and the creature.*

II. Victor Frankenstein's obsession

    A. Curiosity and desire for knowledge:

        1. As a boy, sees lightning strike tree

        2. Study of Agrippa and Paracelsus

    B. Attends University of Ingolstadt:

        1. Influence of M. Waldman

        2. Intensive study and experimentation

        3. Loses contact with family and friends

    C. Creation of a monster:

        1. Ambition blinds him to reality of creation

            a. Thinks creature will be beautiful

        2. Confronted with living creature

        3. Horrified at what he has created

    D. Life destroyed by his creation:

        1. Family and friends killed

        2. No hope for future

        3. Sinks into black hole of anger and revenge

III. The creature's quest for knowledge

    A. Creature as a blank innocent:

        1. Is benevolent, but knows nothing

        2. Wants to be accepted

    B. Is exposed to world of knowledge:

        1. Observation of De Lacey family

        2. Books, music, and loving relationships

        3. Learns to read and write

    C. Desires knowledge and understanding of world:

        1. Reads *Paradise Lost* and other works

        2. Reads Victor's journal

    D. Acquires a terrible knowledge:

        1. Understands who he is and how he was created

        2. Realizes he is doomed to lifelong misery

    E. Becomes obsessed with notion of revenge:

        1. Murders innocent people

        2. Devotes life to torment of Victor

        3. Seeks release in fiery death

IV. Walton's expedition

    A. Walton's obsessive quest:

        1. Like Victor, spends years pursuing dream

    B. Confronted with reality of hardship and pain:

        1. Could destroy crew and himself

    C. Learns from Victor and ultimately abandons quest

V. Conclusion

SECTION FOUR

Bibliography

Baldick, Chris. In *Frankenstein's Shadow: Myth, Monstrosity, and Nineteenth-Century Writing*. Oxford, England: Clarendon Press, 1987.

Bloom, Harold, ed. *Mary Shelley's Frankenstein*. New York: Chelsea House Publishers, 1987.

Kiely, Robert. *The Romantic Novel in England*. Cambridge, MA.: Harvard University Press, 1972.

Nichie, Elizabeth. *Mary Shelley: Author of Frankenstein*. New Brunswick, NJ: Rutgers University Press, 1953.

Shelley, Mary Wollstonecraft. *Frankenstein or, The Modern Prometheus*. Berkeley and Los Angeles: University of California Press, 1984.

Spark, Muriel. *Mary Shelley*. New York: E. P. Dutton, 1987.

Sunstein, Emily W. *Mary Shelley: Romance and Reality*. Boston: Little Brown & Company, 1989.

Vasbinder, Samuel Holmes. *Scientific Attitudes in Mary Shelley's Frankenstein*. Ann Arbor, MI: UMI Research Press, 1984.

Walling, William A. *Mary Shelley*. Boston: Twayne Publishers, 1972.

MAXnotes®

REA's Literature Study Guides

MAXnotes® are student-friendly. They offer a fresh look at masterpieces of literature, presented in a lively and interesting fashion. **MAXnotes®** offer the essentials of what you should know about the work, including outlines, explanations and discussions of the plot, character lists, analyses, and historical context. **MAXnotes®** are designed to help you think independently about literary works by raising various issues and thought-provoking ideas and questions. Written by literary experts who currently teach the subject, **MAXnotes®** enhance your understanding and enjoyment of the work.

Available **MAXnotes®** include the following:

Absalom, Absalom!
The Aeneid of Virgil
Animal Farm
Antony and Cleopatra
As I Lay Dying
As You Like It
The Autobiography of
    Malcolm X
The Awakening
Beloved
Beowulf
Billy Budd
The Bluest Eye, A Novel
Brave New World
The Canterbury Tales
The Catcher in the Rye
The Color Purple
The Crucible
Death in Venice
Death of a Salesman
The Divine Comedy I: Inferno
Dubliners
Emma
Euripedes' Electra & Medea
Frankenstein
Gone with the Wind
The Grapes of Wrath
Great Expectations
The Great Gatsby
Gulliver's Travels
Hamlet
Hard Times

Heart of Darkness
Henry IV, Part I
Henry V
The House on Mango Street
Huckleberry Finn
I Know Why the Caged
    Bird Sings
The Iliad
Invisible Man
Jane Eyre
Jazz
The Joy Luck Club
Jude the Obscure
Julius Caesar
King Lear
Les Misérables
Lord of the Flies
Macbeth
The Merchant of Venice
The Metamorphoses of Ovid
The Metamorphosis
Middlemarch
A Midsummer Night's Dream
Moby-Dick
Moll Flanders
Mrs. Dalloway
Much Ado About Nothing
My Antonia
Native Son
1984
The Odyssey
Oedipus Trilogy

Of Mice and Men
On the Road
Othello
Paradise Lost
A Passage to India
Plato's Republic
Portrait of a Lady
A Portrait of the Artist
    as a Young Man
Pride and Prejudice
A Raisin in the Sun
Richard II
Romeo and Juliet
The Scarlet Letter
Sir Gawain and the
    Green Knight
Slaughterhouse-Five
Song of Solomon
The Sound and the Fury
The Stranger
The Sun Also Rises
A Tale of Two Cities
Taming of the Shrew
The Tempest
Tess of the D'Urbervilles
Their Eyes Were Watching God
To Kill a Mockingbird
To the Lighthouse
Twelfth Night
Uncle Tom's Cabin
Waiting for Godot
Wuthering Heights

RESEARCH & EDUCATION ASSOCIATION
61 Ethel Road W. • Piscataway, New Jersey 08854
Phone: (908) 819-8880

Please send me more information about MAXnotes®.

Name _____

Address _____

City _____ State _____ Zip _____

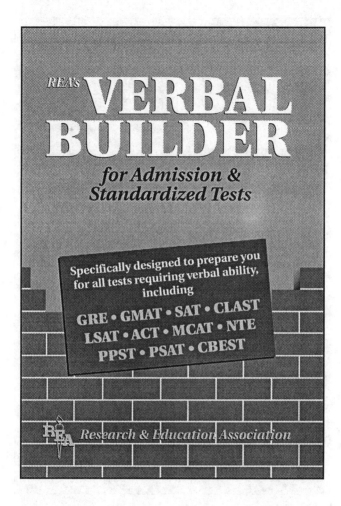

REA's **VERBAL BUILDER**

for Admission & Standardized Tests

Specifically designed to prepare you for all tests requiring verbal ability, including

GRE • GMAT • SAT • CLAST
LSAT • ACT • MCAT • NTE
PPST • PSAT • CBEST

Research & Education Association

Available at your local bookstore or order directly from us by sending in coupon below.